kurz & bündig

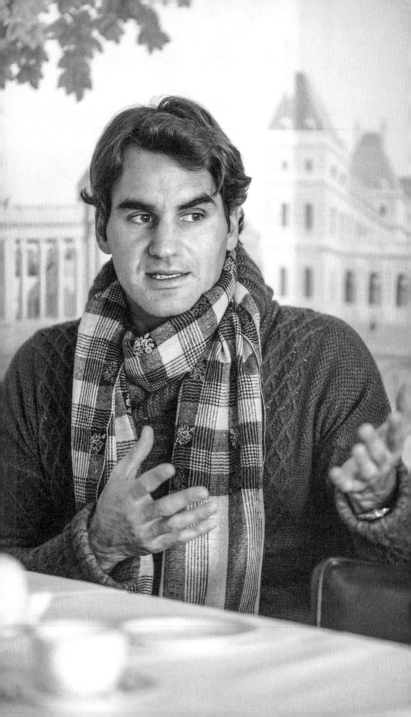

Phenomenon.
Enthusiast.
Philanthropist.

Roger Federer

by Simon Graf

kurz & bündig verlag | **Frankfurt a. M.** | **Basel**

Visit us online:
www.kurz-und-buendig-verlag.com

The production of this book was made possible by

Communication • Translation • Interpretation

Translation by Sophie Hall, Brussels, Belgium.
Proofreading by www.syntax.ch.
Layout by Katja von Ruville, Frankfurt am Main, Germany, based on an
idea by Fanny Oppler, Basel, Switzerland.
Cover and content photographs by Romina Amato.
Page makeup by Katja von Ruville, Frankfurt am Main, Germany.
Printing and binding by CPI books GmbH, Leck, Germany.

Printbook ISBN: 978-3-907126-11-0
ePUB ISBN: 978-3-907126-24-0

Preface

Sometimes, it's simply a matter of luck. When I started re- **5** porting on tennis for the Tages-Anzeiger and the Sonn- tagsZeitung in Zurich, no one could have known that a certain Roger Federer would rewrite the record books, becoming a Swiss national hero and a global icon. I accompanied him on many of his victory tours around the tennis world and grew to know him better through several long, personal interviews. Whether in the garden of his rented house in Wimbledon after his first Grand Slam title in 2003, in his room in a luxury hotel in Geneva, in a cafe on the banks of the River Rhine in Basel or in Lenzerheide in the mountains of the Grisons, where he now lives. In addition, I had exchanges with him in countless press conferences and other media events, listening to him for hundreds of hours. I offer him my warmest thanks for his openness and his willingness to engage on subjects which reach far beyond the court.

The following biography is not authorised. However, over close to 20 years spent writing about Federer, I have been fortunate to learn much about him through conversations with him and with people from his family and sporting life. I can paint a good picture of him. Not just of the athlete, but of the person who, like the rest of us, has had his battles to fight – even if, from the outside, his life seems like a rapid succession of successes. In this book, I try to capture Federer's many sides. A quick-tempered teenager, a tennis genius, a son, husband and father, an inspiration, strategist, manager of his own talent, victorious and defeated, an icon, exceptional athlete, philanthropist and **6** more.

The portrait is not strictly chronological – instead it is a collection of 16 longer, thematically arranged pieces on Federer. It can be read from start to finish, or in whichever order you like. The chapters stand alone, and when you have read them all, the picture is complete.

Kilchberg, 31st of March 2019

1. The people's king

It's a beautiful day in paradise. The sun is shining and a light breeze is blowing through the mountains of Gstaad, making the summer heat bearable. It's the 23rd of July 2013, and the resort town is looking forward to seeing Federer play. The global star hasn't been here for nine years. But in his desperate search for match practice, he's stopping in the Bernese Oberland. They're so delighted that they've given him a cow again – as they had done in 2003, after his first Wimbledon victory. But when I happen to see Federer warming up on the courts of the Gstaad Palace a few hours before his match, I feel a pang of foreboding. I see nothing of the legendary elegance and ease, he seems stiff, robotic. His back is clearly still bothering him. Is it really a good idea to face the German Daniel Brands? No, it isn't, as we learn a few hours later. Federer plays like a poor imitation of himself, seems restrained and soon resigned. After 65 minutes and a 3-6, 4-6 finish he leaves the court with his head bowed.

These are agonising months for Federer. Defending his title in Wimbledon, he fails against Ukrainian unknown Sergiy Stakhovsky in the second round. Throughout 2013, his chronic back issues resurface again and again. After his embarrassing performance in front of the eager home crowds in Gstaad, he's unlikely to be keen to talk about his feelings. But of course he appears at the obligatory press conference and faces the excruciating questions – and there are quite a few. No one could blame him for keeping it short, but he takes questions for half an hour, even though he himself doesn't know what will become of him and his **8** back. And then he even takes the time for a chat with the son of former Swiss pro Claudio Mezzadri and the others who have eagerly waited to meet him for the first time. He swallows his frustrations at an uncooperative body, empathising with those who were so excited to see him. Having disappointed them on the court, he takes all the more time for them off-court. He probably wants nothing more than to leave and take care of himself rather than others. This side story speaks volumes about him.

I could have begun this portrait with descriptions of Federer's magnificent victories. But it's easy for victors to shine. A person's true character only reveals itself in difficult moments. Like that day in the Bernese Oberland, at a low point in his career. Federer has often read the two lines from Rudyard Kipling's "If" inscribed above the entrance to Wimbledon's Centre Court. He knows them by heart:

"If you can meet with Triumph and Disaster
And treat those two impostors just the same"

The poem ends on the words:

"Yours is the Earth and everything that's in it,
And — which is more — you'll be a Man, my son!"

Kipling's 1910 poem was directed at his son John, who would later die whilst serving in the First World War. To this day, it's one of the most popular poems in Britain. Federer embodies the spirit of Kipling's lines. At the very least of those above. For all his wins and titles and his rockstar life, the subject of constant admiration, he has stayed humble. And he refuses to be discouraged by defeats and setbacks.

Federer learned a lot at home, and not just in sporting terms. But the man from rural Basel also rose to the challenge of a life in the limelight and his role as a central figure in the global circus of professional sports. He realised early on that as a beloved player, he is no longer his own man, and that he carries a responsibility towards others. And he bears it, all the while staying true to himself. Whether he wants to or not, Federer shapes other people's lives. Their admiration for him at times borders on the religious. His most loyal fans invest all their holiday days to fly around the world to see him and spend hours making Federer memorabilia, finding inspiration for their own lives in his.

The tradition of the red envelope is by now legendary, reaching back to 2003 when he first won at Wimbledon. Since then, the core group of fans hands him an envelope of good luck notes before each Grand Slam tournament as well as before many other tournaments. For his supporters, the greatest privilege is to be chosen as the courier to hand over the hundred or so messages during pre-tournament training.

To really feel the pulse of the tennis world, you should pitch up a tent in Wimbledon Park in July, during the "All England Championships", stay overnight and try to secure tickets.

10 And then chat to your neighbours about Federer to pass the time. You quickly notice: not everyone with a Swiss flag stuck to their tent, a Swiss cross t-shirt or a baseball cap with "RF" on it is Swiss. The Federer-aficionados come from Calcutta, Shanghai, Melbourne, Dubai, Tennessee, and of course also Basel and London, from every corner of the world. Everyone can tell you the moment they "clicked". There is surely no other athlete who has inspired such an urge to share in his fans, nor so many books in which the authors ponder what the tennis virtuoso has triggered in them.

Whilst sports are usually dismissed as uncool in cultural circles, here, too, Federer has captivated many. In an interview in 2017, German violinist Anne-Sophie Mutter told the Frankfurter Allgemeine Zeitung: "I can't understand how you could be a fan of any other living tennis player once you have seen Federer. You can't help but fall for that beauty, that elegance, that wonderfully poetic style of play." She spoke of how she had arranged her 2014 concerts in Australia so as to be able to see Federer play the final at the Australian Open in Melbourne. Too bad he lost to Nadal in the semi-final.

The five-time World Sportsman of the Year's appeal may be global, but he is decidedly Swiss. According to Torsten Tomczak, Professor of Marketing at the renowned University of St. Gallen, studies on "Swissness" repeatedly turn out characteristics which Federer embodies. Federer stands for the values of both a modern and a traditional Switzerland: he's cosmopolitan, but down-to-earth, hard-working, creative, ambitious, a family man, friendly, but firm, reliable and suitably modest. He doesn't quite cultivate understatement like his rival Rafael Nadal, but also never crosses the line between confidence and arrogance. And, like Switzerland, he is neutral. Federer is the perfect diplomat, never publicly airing his views on sensitive issues. It's a smart strategy at a time when journalists are hungrier than ever for a sensational headline to be shared a thousand times over social media.

There's probably no other athlete who's been interviewed as often as Federer. There have been over 1,400 post-match press conferences alone. Under that kind of scrutiny, there's no hiding for long. His consistency was underlined by a survey conducted by the American Reputation Institute in 2011. Fifty thousand people were asked to rank 54 public personalities from politics, culture, business and sports on the degree to which they are liked, admired, respected and trusted. Federer came in second, just behind the now deceased Nobel Peace Prize winner Nelson Mandela, but ahead of figures like the Dalai Lama, Barack Obama and Bill Gates. In 2017, he was also awarded an honorary PhD from the Medical Faculty of the University of

Basel for promoting the reputations of both Basel and Switzerland across the world, for his presence as a sporting role model, and for his involvement in his foundation's work with children in South Africa.

What's most astounding is how much his competitors like him, even though he almost always beats them. From 2004 to 2017 he won the Stefan Edberg Sportsmanship Award for fairness and integrity 13 times – on election by his fellow players. It was snatched away just once in that period, by Nadal, in 2010. This annual award should also be seen as the other tennis stars' thanks for changing the atmosphere of the professional tennis circuit for good. Whilst the former number ones like Pete Sampras or Andre Agassi tended to make themselves scarce and goad the competition, Federer mingles with everyone – no matter how old or young, good or bad they are. Perhaps a mark of his Swiss upbringing. Although he's often called a (tennis) king, he's a king of the people – in the changing room or players' lounge, he's stayed just one of the guys, unreserved and always up for a joke. His straightforwardness has relaxed the atmosphere on the men's tour: "I always found it best to be nice to the new generation of players rather than making them feel it would be hell for them here," Federer once said. "I think that rubbed off on Nadal and the other players. Of course tennis is a tough sport, but it's still a sport. There are more important things in life."

His friendly, personable attitude, however, doesn't mean he tries to please everyone. He has always gone his own way and taken hard decisions when he felt they were necessary. Like the decision to part from several coaches, not to participate in the Davis Cup or to withdraw from the whole clay court season twice. And on the court he certainly knows no mercy. One of those who has suffered the most at his hand in sporting terms is Andy Roddick. They have faced each other in eight Grand Slam tournaments, and Federer won eight times – four of those in the final. After the Wimbledon final in 2005, Roddick turned to Federer and put it in a nutshell: "I'd love to hate you, but you're really nice."

2. Does the apple fall far from the tree?

A chance encounter often says more about a person than **14** a wordy description. The former doubles specialist Eric Butorac has a telling story about Lynette Federer, Roger's mother.

Butorac, Federer's American successor as president of the Player Council from 2014–2016, was never much of a bigwig as a player. Certainly not in 2006, when he did the rounds in the doubles' competitions of the second-rate Challenger Tour. In October that year, he also stopped at the Swiss Indoors Basel, bringing along his coach. Not because he thought he had much of a shot, but because he wanted to see Roger Federer live. After being knocked out in the second round, he and his coach hurried to the main arena, where the local hero was playing David Ferrer. Their players' badges got them access to the stadium, but there were no more seats left in the stands. An usher suggested they try their luck in the sponsor boxes. They got lucky, spotting two free seats in a box in the front row, and snuck in after three games. The other four people in the box of six didn't seem to mind. The "older woman", as Butorac describes her in his blog, was actually extremely welcoming, "peppering me with questions about my own tennis career. Where was

I from? Which racket did I use? What was my ranking? ... were only a few of her curiosities."

After three or four games of conversation, Butorac wanted to finally concentrate on the match. He was there for Federer, after all. But since he was a guest in a sponsor's box, he felt obliged to make conversation before he could get back to business in good conscience. So he asked the older woman: "So, is your company a sponsor of the tournament?" She replied: "Sponsor? Oh no, this isn't a sponsor box. It's a personal box." Butorac was confused: "... personal box?" She explained: "Why yes... I am Roger's mother. And (gesturing) – this is his father, his sister, and his agent..." The doubles player was hopelessly embarrassed to have snuck onto these exclusive seats. But Lynette Federer chatted away. "Do you know Roger? Are you guys friends?" His father Robert joined the conversation, but the bashful intruder was suddenly shy and tongue-tied. He was so uncomfortable that he could barely wait for the match to end. "It felt like the longest straight-set, Roger-in-his-prime, victory that I have ever witnessed." He felt like a little child who'd raided the biscuit tin. After the match he dashed out of the arena to avoid meeting Federer himself. That evening has stayed with him. Even though he was a total stranger, the Federer box treated him like an old friend.

Two years later at the US Open, just as he was packing after losing at mixed doubles, José Higueras, Federer's coach at the time, asked him if he was already leaving. He nodded. "OK, that's too bad, I was just looking for a lefty to practise with Roger tomorrow." Of course, Butorac wasn't about to throw away this opportunity: "Did I say today? Sorry, I meant I was leaving tomorrow." And so he got to know Federer himself, before later becoming his friend as his vice-president in the Player Council. He says of Federer: "I've seen him give more time and effort than are required to sponsors and fans, and I've seen him handle even the most invasive, uncourteous requests with unwavering grace. Some might think he puts on a show for the public, but that's just who he is." He's been asked countless times whether Federer is really that nice. He always replies: "No, he's nicer!" and that he knows where he gets it from. His parents. Many of Federer's character traits really can be attributed to his parents: his down-to-earth but cosmopolitan nature, his consistency, his fairness, his strong family values, his humour and his sociable nature.

Lynette and Robert Federer grew up 11,000 kilometres apart: her in Kempton Park, a large South African city near Johannesburg, and him in Berneck in the Rhine Valley of St. Gallen. It's an idyllic village of around 4,000 people, and on the wall of the town hall there hangs a bust of Federer – Heinrich Federer. Like the athlete, the poet (1866–1928) was officially a citizen of Berneck, but never actually lived there. Looking at the bust and its striking nose sideways, you could almost suspect that the two men must be distantly related. Robert Federer was raised in one of the oldest houses in Berneck and grew up helping out on the fields in the surrounding countryside. He was trained as a lab technician in the (now closed) Viscosuisse factory in nearby Widnau, where his father was a shift worker producing synthetic fibre. But he soon felt the pull of the wider world. First Basel, where he started at Ciba, and then, at 24 years old, South Africa, where he went to work for the same Swiss chemicals company. In 1970, he met 18-year-old secretary Lynette Durand in the staff canteen. They fell in love and became a couple. The youngest of four children, she had always dreamed of moving to England. Instead, she moved to Basel with Robert in 1973, where they married and continued to work for the same company, now called **17** Ciba-Geigy. In 1979, their daughter Diana was born, and, on the 8th of August 1981, Roger.

Lynette Federer grew up in a cosmopolitan family – she has a French name and surname (Durand), but also German and Dutch roots. At home they spoke Afrikaans, but having gone to an English school at her father's suggestion, she speaks the Queen's English. Once in Basel, she quickly learned Swiss German, easing her integration. Multilingualism later also became one of Roger Federer's trademarks. Even though his father Robert left Berneck more than fifty years ago, you can still hear the St. Gallen roots in his dialect. It's no coincidence that many successful sportsmen like Federer have a multicultural background. But if an extraordinary athlete were drafted at the drawing board, Lynette and Roger Federer would hardly have been the obvious choice of parents. Both are on the short side, if anything, and neither is a particularly exceptional athlete. But they noticed early on that their son had strong coordination skills. At 11 months, he could already walk on his own, Lynette told the Basler Zeitung in an interview for his 30th

» Many of Federer's character traits really can be attributed to his parents: his down-to-earth but cosmopolitan nature, his consistency, his fairness, his strong family values, his humour and his sociable nature. «

birthday. Maybe thanks to the "giant feet" he already had at birth. "He was quickly playing football and catching balls," says Robert. "We played with him constantly − football, ping pong, later squash. There are lovely photos of him just peering over the top of the ping-pong table." Lynette adds: "We always had a ball with us at the playground. You could send over a ball and it came straight back, whilst the other kids scattered them all over the place."

20   When asked what he has inherited from his parents, Federer says: "In terms of tennis, it's hard to say, since they both learned fairly late. And you can see that. Maybe athleticism. My mother played hockey and did ballet. And my father? He hiked in Appenzell. I think I had fairly normal starting conditions." Lynette is the more athletic of the two. In South Africa, she made it into a regional hockey selection − but stopped because of the many hits to the shins. Robert had little time for sports when he was young. He played football from time to time and ended up with FC Widnau at 17 or 18, before leaving for the big wide world. He only discovered tennis at 24. When he met Lynette, it became their shared hobby: first in the Swiss Club in Johannesburg, and later, after they moved to Switzerland, on Ciba-Geigy's company grounds in Allschwil.

Although they learned to play late, both reached an impressive level. Despite holding a racket in her hand for the first time aged 19, Lynette even became Swiss national champion in 1995 with the over 30s of Tennis Club Old Boys Basel. They say she had a "toxic slice". That shot seems to be genetic. Speaking of genes: "Roger probably has his gaming instinct from me," his mother suspects. "I was very ambitious, I always had this urge to win. I never let him win as a little boy. Not even in the football games we had in the hall outside the kitchen after lunch every day when he was at primary school. It was always a serious business. It was a fight every day and we never let each other off easy." But for all her ambition she always played fair – which also left its mark on him. Put simply, Roger inherited his mother's playfulness and his father's grounded nature. That's not to say that Robert doesn't get emotional sometimes. After all these years and victories, he can still get worked up if his son misses an easy forehand. That's why Robert and Lynette prefer not to sit next to each other in the stands when Roger plays. Although in the Royal Box in Centre Court at Wimbledon it can't always be avoided. "My wife doesn't want to sit next to me," he smiles. "It's just nicer that way," she explains. Her husband's comments are hard to handle if she is feeling tense. Federer says of his parents: "My father has a tough shell and a soft heart. My mother is more balanced."

In the beginning it was Lynette who took Roger to the court, later Robert became the more active supporter of his son's tennis career. Although Lynette ran junior practice at Tennis Club Ciba, she resisted teaching little Roger. The parents placed their trust in experienced coaches early on and stayed out of things. But it mattered to them that he showed the necessary commitment to his hobby. Federer relates: "My father often said to me: 'I think it's good that you play tennis and enjoy it. But please, when you train, take it seriously. It's expensive.' My mother thought the same, but said it less directly." Between 13 and 17, his parents spent around CHF 30,000 a year on their son's tennis career. A tidy sum. To get the money together, Lynette increased her hours to work almost full-time. When Robert Federer was made a tempting offer of a job in Australia, the family decided to stay in Switzerland, amongst other things, for the good training available for Roger.

22 Despite all the sacrifices the parents made, they didn't put their son under pressure. The decision to move to the national training centre in Ecublens, far from the familiarity of his home, friends and language region, at 14 was his own. It paid off that the parents had fostered their children's independence early. They had had no choice, says Lynette. Robert spent much time abroad with work, his parents were in Eastern Switzerland and Lynette's family were far away in South Africa. The children learned early to cycle to training or school on their own. This high degree of autonomy marked Roger and shaped the later tennis pro Federer. He doesn't shy away from decisions, whether on or off the court. He never looks longingly at his box, hoping for a signal from his coach. He looks for his own solutions.

Federer gained independence from his parents early, but their relationship remains close. They play an active role in his professional career. After he ended his relationship with the US marketing giant IMG in 2003, he even temporarily opted for family management. Lynette left Ciba after 33 years to look after her son professionally. In 2005, he then returned to IMG – having become a six-time Grand Slam champion. To this day, his family are heavily involved in their son's activities, whether as board members of the Roger Federer Foundation, in replying to fan mail and much more. That he wants them there at as many tournaments as possible shows that they did an awful lot right. "The fact that my parents are so proud of me is motivating," he says. "And it makes me happy that they enjoy coming to matches." Father Robert says: "The biggest compliment for us is to see the welcome he gets in the stadium. Even if he's playing Gaël Monfils in France or Andy Murray in England. It's why I usually go into the stadium five minutes before him."

The father follows each match as eagerly as ever, but he's been able to overcome the superstition that he brings Roger bad luck. After sitting in the stands during the terrible first-round defeat against Mario Ančić in Wimbledon in 2002, he stayed away from the All England Club for the following two years. And ended up missing his son's first Wimbledon win. Speaking to the tabloid The Sun on the phone, he explained to a baffled reporter that he had had to feed the cat. You can imagine the twinkle of mischief in his eyes, serving up that little white lie.

»The fact his love for tennis didn't change when he wasn't winning so often is an homage to the sport in its purest form.«

3. The birth of a champion

26 Dark clouds hang over the All England Lawn Tennis and Croquet Club on this Monday, the 30th of June 2003. They stand for the trouble brewing for Federer in the fourth round at Wimbledon against Feliciano López. The player from Basel is there to deliver on the promise of his immense talent and his 2001 coup against Pete Sampras. Suddenly, during the warm-up, a shooting pain runs through his back.

Anyone who's ever swung a racket knows that in this sport of swivels and turns there is nothing more unpleasant than a blocked back. If only it would start to rain again, he thinks. Then he could go back to the locker rooms, be treated, take painkillers and wait for them to kick in. But on this grey day, even the British weather fails him. It stays dry. The sporting drama plays out on Court 2, also known as the "Graveyard of Champions". Many a player has left the intimate little court misty-eyed. This was where Sampras' Wimbledon career had ended the year before. Against George Bastl, the journeyman from the Swiss resort town of Villars-sur-Ollon who had failed to qualify but slipped into the competition after a cancellation – only to beat the seven-time champion. No one would have wished such an exit on Sampras on the site of his greatest victories. In the changeovers, he had returned to his chair to read and re-read a letter from his wife Bridgette, who had written him words of encouragement. To no avail. And now it seemed the "graveyard" was to claim its next victim.

So many were rooting for the young Swiss player with the ponytail and the elegant style of play to have his break-through on tennis's greatest stage. After the era of Pete Sampras and Andre Agassi, the sport was hungry for new stars. The men's tour had launched a campaign called "New balls please" for a reason. Federer looked down from the poster with dark resolve — next to other aspiring players like Andy Roddick, Lleyton Hewitt, Marat Safin and Juan Carlos Ferrero. But somehow the tennis virtuoso never seemed to get it together at Grand Slam tournaments. He had failed in the first round at three of his last five starts. A few weeks ago, in Paris, to Peruvian Luis Horna, number 88 in the world. Federer seemed paralysed. The French sports paper L'Équipe wrote: "You felt the urge to go down onto the court and shake the man out of his daydream."

Was he thinking of that disappointment in those un-easy moments on Court 2 at Wimbledon? When, after two games, he called the physiotherapist and was treated on the side of the court, a murmur went through the stands. Would he play on? During the five-minute break, the 21-year-old thought about conceding. But then he thought better of it. It helped that his opponent, whose muscular build and long hair make him look like a Roman gladiator, was blessed with significantly less tactical intelligence. The

Spanish left-hander couldn't quite capitalise on Federer's limitations enough, playing hastily instead of drawing him into long rallies. And although Federer had to slow down his serve by about 6 mph to spare his back, he stayed comfortable in his serve.

He only won three more points but got through after three tight sets. His Swedish coach Peter Lundgren finally caught his breath. It was only six days later, a beaming Wimbledon champion, that Federer described how he really felt against López: "I was really in big pain. I was struggling to serve, I was struggling to return. I couldn't even really sit down because I was hurting so much. Then I called the trainer after two games and he gave me painkillers, he gave me a massage on my back with warm cream. And I told myself, 'If this continues for a few more games, and I realised that this guy was just kicking my ass, it's not worth playing.' But somehow I stayed in the match and it got a little bit better."

His win in that turbulent fourth round at Church Road is only a footnote. But for him, it was a major step. The British weather reared its head again on Wednesday and forced back his quarter final to Thursday, a boon not only to Federer's back but also to his opponent. Sjeng Schalken had had to have a hematoma on his left foot surgically removed and could barely walk. But two days off and intravenous painkillers still weren't enough for the Dutchman: he was still constrained and didn't stand a chance. Suddenly, only two victories stood between Federer and his first Grand Slam title. Years later, Federer admits that in the four great tournaments of Melbourne, Paris, Wimbledon and New York, he was held back by the thought of having to win seven best-of-five matches to claim these prestigious titles. He saw an Everest before him, and the thought of climbing it was dizzying.

But suddenly, the peak is within sight. It's as if his back pain has melted away, together with his doubts. Before the semi-final against Andy Roddick he no longer worries about the American's serve, which regularly thunders across the court at 125 mph. "He won't hit 200 aces," he says. In the clash of the two young stars, he is in the zone. Roddick is amazed by his opponent, to whom it all comes easily, he wrangles with his fate, begins to doubt himself – and finally retreats into gallows humour.

Federer sends inch-perfect volleys into the corner, is always one step ahead, and usually senses the right corner to receive Roddick's serve. The devastating number for the challenger from Omaha, Nebraska, one year his junior: Federer serves 17 aces over three sets; he manages just four. Even rallies in which he had played well, he ended up losing the point, Roddick later notes, shaking his head. Coach Peter Lundgren, who had until then been rather critical of Federer's performances at the All England Club, speaks of his protégé in the highest tones. This was the best he had ever seen him play, said the Swede. As a commentator on the BBC, Becker waxes lyrical: "Every child who wants to learn tennis should watch Federer. He is rewriting the textbook. We have witnessed the birth of a new age." Not quite. After all, there's one more match to go: the final against Mark Philippoussis. After three knee operations – even spending two and a half months in a wheelchair – the 26-year-old Australian has managed an impressive come-back. In Wimbledon, the 6 ft 5 in giant had, amongst others, beaten the number one Andre Agassi with his sheer power – he's nicknamed "scud", like the rocket, for a reason.

But after his brilliant performance against Roddick, Federer begins his great match as the favourite.

30   The 6th of July 2003 will go down in Swiss sporting history. "The Harry Potter of tennis" (The Times) waves his wand, the magic lasts less than two hours. Once it's done, once 7-6, 6-2, 7-6 stands, Federer falls to his knees and looks up to his girlfriend Mirka Vavrinec and coach Lundgren in his box. During the match he had kept his nerves and opponent under control, now he is overcome with emotion. As he sits in his chair, waiting to receive the trophy, slowly realising what he has achieved, he cries for the first time. Holding the golden trophy as gently as if it were a newborn, he bravely struggles through the win-ner's interview. His words and thoughts are rambling, he wavers between arrogance and emotion. When, in his enthusiasm, he lets slip that he likes to watch himself, too, he smiles at himself. In the end he bursts into tears again, and with him many in the stadium and in front of the television.

"It's Roger Blubberer," declared London tabloid Daily Mirror in a merciless headline. The broadsheets composed artful elegies after the Swiss player's victory. Renowned tennis journalist John Parsons wrote in the Daily Telegraph:

"Take the ice-cool Wimbledon temperament of Björn Borg, add the elegant volleying skills of Stefan Edberg, stir with the serving authority of Pete Sampras and the returning qualities of Andre Agassi and there you have a taste of the new Wimbledon champion, Roger Federer. (...) The final day reached a fitting climax with the triumph going to a young man who could become a giant among champions." Paris sports paper L'Équipe, which had just weeks ago derided him, was full of praise: "Blessed with extraordinary talent and a refreshingly straightforward personality, he is the ideal ambassador of this beautiful sport. In these turbulent times, the success of this artist and exemplary young man is the most wonderful news for men's tennis. Sampras can happily retire, his legacy is in good hands." These lines were to prove prophetic.

After a short night following the champions' dinner at the Savoy, Federer greeted the journalists in the garden of his rented house on Monday morning. Number 10, Lake Road, three minutes' drive from the All England Club. He posed, the newspapers and headlines spread out on the table before him, and seemed remarkably fresh. In the moments after the final he had felt anything other than fresh, he said. "After the award ceremony I came back to the locker rooms and was completely drained. My muscles were so tense from the pressure." Then he spoke with the detachment of one much older than his 21 years. "The winners stay, the losers go. Winners and losers are so close together and yet so far from one another. Real champions are those who win. That might sound a bit arrogant, given that

I've just won Wimbledon. But that's just how it is. I wasn't going to give up my chance."

And he explained why his emergence as a champion took time: "What mattered for me was that I could find myself. That I felt at ease inside. I'm the type, the player, the person who has to go through that. A Hewitt or a Safin had more mental strength much earlier. I just took my time." He said he's aware that as a Wimbledon winner, a new life of celebrity will begin. But he's OK with that. "My birth sign is Leo, like Pete Sampras, and we like to be in the centre of attention. So I'm comfortable I'll be able to handle it. And thankfully the paparazzi in Switzerland aren't as bad as in England."

That same day, a private jet takes him to the Bernese mountains, to Gstaad. A clay court competition at 3,445 ft above sea level is pretty much the last thing his exhausted body needs. But Federer doesn't want to disappoint Jacques "Köbi" Hermenjat – after all, the tournament director had given him a wildcard for his first appearance at a professional tournament in 1998, when Federer was just 16. On Tuesday, Hermenjat surprises the freshly-baked champion with a voluptuous gift: an 1,800 lbs Simmental dairy cow named Juliette. The picture of the unlikely pair goes around the world.

The cow as a reward for Federer is in keeping with the homage to him and to Switzerland which The Times of London published after his triumph. A tongue-in-cheek tour d'horizon which deployed every cliché, making reference also to balloonist Bertrand Piccard and the coup of the sailing yacht Alinghi at the Americas Cup: "Sound the alpen-horns and all the other clichés. Let all the cuckoo clocks sing out. Yodel the good news from peak to peak and break open the Toblerone. Roger Federer's victory at Wimbledon has confirmed the Swiss as a nation of sporting heroes, a land where giants emerge from the mountain fastness to sail the seas, balloon around the globe and swashbuckle their way to grassy tennis fame. (...) The men and women who bobbed and slalomed their way to winter victories now are **33** conquering sports far from their landlocked nation's snowy horizons."

4. The hothead finds his zen

34   Tennis is a simple game. Unless you're the one playing. The potential for frustration is considerable. You're constantly forced to make split-second decisions and improvise. And between the rallies and games you have an awful lot of time to think about what you should have done differently. If, like young Roger Federer, you're pursuing perfection, you cannot but fall short of your own expectations. Tempers rise and need an outlet. Thankfully, as a tennis player, there's a racket in your hands that you can take it out on.

   The story of how a teenage Federer ripped the new curtains separating the courts at the tennis academy in Biel is legendary. "I looked at the curtain and thought that it was so thick that there was no way anybody could wreck it," the rueful offender told TV documentary "Replay". "Ten minutes later, I turned around and hurled my racket at the curtain like a helicopter. It sliced through the curtain like a knife going through butter. Everybody stopped playing and stared at me. No, I thought, that's impossible! The worst nightmare!" He packed up his things and left − he would have been thrown out anyway. He had been explicitly warned about damaging the curtains. As punishment, he spent a week cleaning the toilets and offices and preparing the courts between 6 and 7 in the morning. For a boy far from a morning person and years away from the real world of parenting, it was the ultimate punishment.

His first coach, the Czech Adolf "Seppli" Kacovsky, had to contend with the young boy's quick temper early on. And in his biography "The Roger Federer Story: Quest For Perfection", the Swiss journalist René Stauffer, who knew Federer early on, remembers the lasting impression the tal- **35** ented junior made on him when he saw him for the first time – aged 15, at the World Youth Cup in Zurich. It wasn't just Federer's talent which struck him, but also how furious and uncontrolled his behaviour was between rallies. "On several occasions, he threw his racket across the court in anger and disgust. He constantly berated himself. 'Du-ubel!' or 'Idiot!' he exclaimed when one of his balls narrowly missed the line. He sometimes even criticised himself aloud when he actually won points but was dissatisfied with his stroke. He didn't seem to notice what was going on around him. It was only him, the ball, the racket – and his fuming temper – nothing else."

His parents often found it embarrassing. "We were never angry at Roger if he lost a match," his mother Lynette says, "but often because of his behaviour on the court." Robert adds: "Sometimes we felt really ashamed." In 2016, Roger tells a story from his younger years, when his father left the court in frustration at his fits of anger: "He said: 'I don't enjoy playing with you like that.' So he put five Swiss francs on the bench next to me and said, 'I'm leav-

»He doesn't practise yoga or tai-chi, doesn't meditate, or go to shiatsu therapy. Nevertheless, he serves as an example for mindfulness.«

ing, I'll see you at home.' And I couldn't believe he left me there because it was going to be like a 45-minute bus ride back home. So I waited for like an hour until he came back and he never showed up. And I realised he had actually left when I checked the car park…" Another time, Robert stopped the car on a mountain pass on their way home from a junior tournament. His son was still fuming about the match when his father pulled him out of the car and stuck his head in the snow – to cool his hot head. His mother Lynette would say to Roger: "Your bad behaviour is like sending an invitation to your opponent. Saying: Here I am, beat me! I'm really beatable today. Go ahead!" But these lessons and words had little effect at the time.

Federer's temper continued to turn heads during his first few years on the professional circuit. Losing against the Spaniard Alex Corretja in three straight sets in the round of sixteen of Roland Garros in 2000, for example, he hurled his racket away four times within just one game. There is, of course, a YouTube compilation of it. In Rome, in 2001, against Marat Safin, also not the most level-headed, he and the Russian competed in abusing their rackets. After the second set, several scenes were played on the big screen. Federer briefly looked up and saw that it wasn't the successful shots, but rather their explosions which were being shown. "How he got angry and then I got angry. Him, me, him, me, him, me," he says in "Years of Glory", the book about the story of Swiss tennis success. Federer continues: "I saw this and was embarrassed. I thought, now this is really not necessary. The bigger the stage became, the more I realised just how important respect and manners are. Some experiences you just have to make."

From age 17 to 19 he saw Basel sports psychologist Christian Marcolli. Although Federer was still hot-headed and uncontrolled, Marcolli could already see that the potential star was also mentally and emotionally gifted. On the one hand because of his passion for the sport: each defeat felt personal, spurring him on to do anything to prevent them in the future. On the other because of his learning capacity: it was astounding, says Marcolli, how quickly he could digest and deploy new information. Federer never spoke about his work with the sports psychologist in any detail, only touching on it during a press conference at the 2009 clay court tournament in Monte Carlo. "It was more like anger management," he said. It was the only time in his career that he saw a psychologist: "I pretty quickly realised it was basically up to me and not someone else to tell me how to behave, because my parents were telling me anyway, friends as well. Other players were saying, what is wrong with you? It was just up to me to decide when I wanted to take that step and say, you know what, let's try the quiet version of the Roger Federer."

Many see the death of his former coach, Peter Carter, on the 1st of August 2002 (see Chapter 5) as the trigger for his transformation into "Mr Cool". But the process began much earlier. That sort of mental transformation doesn't happen overnight; Federer first had to find a new identity on the court. For a while, he was even too calm. "Most of the greats are spirited," says Heinz Günthardt, the Swiss tennis pioneer and former coach of Steffi Graf. "That energy matters. It drives you. But you have to learn how to handle the inner fire. And there's no question that there's a fire blazing in Federer. Otherwise you could never have a career of that length. He knew how to keep that flame alive." So the question is: how do you release that energy without getting burned?

Stan Wawrinka, for example, the other Swiss Grand Slam champion, plays better when he airs his anger, destroys a racket and smashes it over his knee. (Careful: do not try this at home! Wawrinka is a rare master of this art, too!) Whenever Jimmy Connors felt uncomfortable, he started speaking to the crowds to draw inspiration. Rebel John McEnroe had to get angry, ideally at a referee or linesman, in order to work himself up into a fury for the match. Young Federer's anger, however, was almost always counterproductive, directed at himself rather than others. And wrangling with yourself makes you a poorer, not a better player.

"I was an emotional guy," he says, looking back during the draw ceremony for the Australian Open in early 2018. "I liked to cry after having lost matches, throw my racket, commentate after every shot that I missed. It was just an emotional time. Coming on tour and having the pressure of wanting to do so well it eats you up a little bit. I just thought: I can't have a career like this. Or I will be a wreck by the time I am 25. I wanna enjoy myself on the tour. It's supposed to be this dream come true. I think playing in front of live audiences and live TV helped me to relax a little bit. I wanted to be known to be mentally strong. I was able to turn that around thankfully. I am very happy I went through this whole process. That was just me. I was a bit crazy, but in a good sense, I believe."

The more successful Federer became, the quieter and more controlled he was on the court. Or vice-versa. His mastery was complete when, in Wimbledon in 2003, he almost casually raced to the title on the way to his first Grand Slam success. His transformation is one of the most remark- able in tennis: from the hot-head who embarrassed his parents to the perfect ambassador for the sport. His mother Lynette's words of warning took effect after all. It's clear just how right she was now that her son no longer shows his opponents what's going on inside. He puts on a poker face, showing little more than a twinge of emotion after each point he wins. It's frustrating for his counterparts, who want nothing more than to be able to read his face or gestures. To know that they're managing to rile him.

But Federer stays cool, exuding a calm confidence. He navigates through turbulent matches with the ease of an experienced pilot. And by staying cool-headed, he almost always makes the right decisions, even at critical moments. In a rapid game like tennis, where you often rely on instinct and a few balls lie between victory and defeat, this can make the difference. It became a Federer trademark that the more crucial the point, the better he plays. In his most successful periods, you can count on an ace down the middle on his opponent's break point. And so for years, victories in tight matches – decided by just a few points – could almost be taken for granted. "The big thing with Roger is: he doesn't beat himself," says Australian tennis strategy analyst Craig O'Shannessy. "A lot of the other players get angry, they get mad, they get upset and defeat themselves. Roger took that off the table. He used to be like that early in his career. Not anymore. Other players throw their rackets, they give in, they go for too much. Roger doesn't. He doesn't beat himself. That wins you a lot of matches."

42   A hot-headed teenager, he discovered his zen, although he doesn't use any particular relaxation methods. He doesn't practise yoga or tai-chi, doesn't meditate, or go to shiatsu therapy. Nevertheless, he serves as an example for mindfulness, for staying in the moment and not allowing yourself to be distracted by anything else. Something which, in a hectic, ever more fast-paced world, everyone is looking for. A good example for Federer's ability to focus on the essential are the ATP Finals in 2003, which took place for the first time in Houston: self-made millionaire James McIngvale, dubbed "Mattress Mack", who made his money with his furniture shops, had brought the tournament onto his doorstep. But the conditions at the Westside Tennis Club were far from ideal. Federer presumed to criticise the uneven courts and insufficient training conditions. At one point, he was even forced to train on a court without a net. When McIngvale, who wasn't used to being criticised, caught wind of Federer's comments he was seething with anger. He stormed into the locker rooms and laid into him just as he was preparing for his match against Andre Agassi. Briefly annoyed, Federer gathered himself quickly, was even spurred on by the telling-off. He beat Agassi, who the patriotic McIngvale was rooting for, not once but twice: first in the group stage, then in the final. And "Mattress Mack" had no choice but to congratulate him. After all, the winner is always right.

When Federer began to lose more often, he was criticised for being too calm, for not really fighting defeat. Commentators urged him to clench his fists and shout "Come on!" more often. Mats Wilander even said that he felt like Federer just wanted to play and not even really to win. The Swede's surprising analysis is so often enriching, but for once he was just plain wrong. In spring 2009, the unimaginable happened in Miami: after a missed forehand in the semi-final against Novak Djoković, Federer smashes his racket! The audience whistled as he returned to the bench to fetch a new one. "Is this how a young person's role model should behave?" the Swiss tabloid Blick asked with indignation. "A very poor image of Roger Federer," scolded the broadsheet Neue Zürcher Zeitung. It was his first public act of destruction in five years. But this incident didn't mark a return from Paul to Saul – it just shows that deep down, Federer's fire still rages. And how astonishing it is that it surfaces so rarely.

There's an interesting parallel with Björn Borg, Federer's captain in Team Europe at the Laver Cup and someone he very much admires. Borg, who earned the nickname "Ice-Borg" for his on-court poker face, was a hot-tempered young player, too. He swore, threw rackets, cheated. Borg behaved so horrendously that at 12, he was banned by the

Swedish association for six months. He was also stopped from training in his local tennis club in Södertälje – a formative experience which served as a lesson. After this, he put his emotions in a box, locked it up and threw away the key. He barely allowed himself positive feelings. "Whenever he came off court, if you were in the locker room, you could never tell whether he'd won or lost," describes his former rival Ilie Năstase. "He'd come in, peel off those tight Fila outfits he wore, fold them into a neat pile, and shuffle off to the showers."

Whilst Borg suppressed every emotion, Federer channels his. After great victories and bitter defeats they resurface, often through his tears. He normalised crying in men's tennis. After losing the final of the Australian Open to him in 2010, Andy Murray offered an honest and moving speech on the court: "I can cry like Roger. It's just a shame I can't play like him."

5. Peter Carter is always there – Federer's coaches

It's no coincidence that Federer's classical style and ease re- semble those of former Australian greats like Rod Laver or Ken Rosewall. His first coach was Czech Adolf "Seppli" Kacovsky. But his most influential one was an Australian from the Barossa Valley, famous for its wines (in particular Shiraz): Peter Carter. Roger was nine when his mother introduced him to the popular blond coach. Carter, a club player and coach at Tennis Club Old Boys Basel, had long noticed the talented firebrand. That night he called his parents and said, "I have a good one here." Though technically strong, the slender Australian had never quite managed a breakthrough on the professional circuit. His best ranking was 173, and from his mid-twenties he focused on his job as a coach. And with Federer, he took on quite a responsibility. "You could see Roger's talent immediately," he said a few years later in an interview in the Basler Zeitung. "He could quickly do a lot with a racket and ball. He was very playful and mostly wanted to have fun. At one point I wondered if he would ever be more concentrated. He has been since he was about 13."

Federer was a natural with the ball. His forehand was

his forte early on, whilst his one-handed backhand was his weak spot. Darren Cahill, a good friend of Carter's and one of the most well-regarded professional coaches – leading Lleyton Hewitt and Andre Agassi to number one and most recently Simona Halep to her first Grand Slam title – described his first impression of Federer in a column for Fox Sports. Carter had raved about the Swiss boy, but when Cahill saw the 13-year-old play during a visit to Basel, he was disappointed. Yes, the boy had a quick arm and a good feel for the ball, but he was a little incomplete for Cahill. He disliked his backhand in particular. "Whaddya think of him?" Carter asked, stepping from the court. "He looks OK," Cahill replied. "That's it, just OK?" And then Cahill listed every flaw he saw in Federer's backhand. "Carts, you could drive a bus through that backhand. Look at that thing. He shanks it half the time, his slice sits up, he takes a huge step when it's outside the slot and he's not stepping to the left on the neutral ball." But Carter was not to be discouraged: "Yeah, but he's gonna be good, isn't he?"

Cahill was convinced that a boy from Adelaide had a better shot. When he saw Federer again two years later at the World Youth Cup in Zurich, Federer faced that boy: Lleyton Hewitt. Cahill expected Hewitt to exploit his Swiss opponent's backhand and win easily. But the stroke had improved significantly in the meantime. In a heated match of thrown rackets and furious rants, Federer won in three sets. Carter was right.

At 14, Federer moved to the national training centre of Ecublens by Lake Geneva, where school and training were brought under one roof, and the partnership with Carter was put on hold for two years. But with Tennis Club Old Boys Basel, they played in the top league together. In August 1997, Swiss Tennis moved the Australian to the newly opened House of Tennis in Biel, and charged him with looking after Federer for the association. The two travelled together often, and in 1998, Federer won the Junior Championships at Wimbledon. The teenager became more and more professional, and in the spring of 2000, Carter himself learned how much he was willing to go his own way – painfully so. Having made it into the top 50 in the world, the next logical step for Federer was to separate from Swiss Tennis and continue with a private coach. But rather than Carter, who had invested so much time in him, he opted for Peter Lundgren. Carter couldn't hide his disappointment. The decision was a difficult one for Federer, but he refused to let his good personal relationship with Carter get in the way of his career. He felt that Lundgren's experience on the global tennis stage made him the better choice. The long-haired Swede, hailed in his youth as "the new Björn Borg", had reached number 25 in the world and had on good days beaten champions like Pete Sampras, Andre Agassi, Mats Wilander and Ivan Lendl. But he had had quite a few bad days, too.

With Lundgren at his side, Federer continued his rise, reaching the top 10 for the first time in 2002. But he hadn't forgotten Carter and pushed for him to become the Swiss Davis Cup captain. But the Australian, who saw the position as a great honour, could only carry it out once – in February

2002, in Moscow, where two Federer wins weren't quite enough for a victory. At the beginning of August, when Federer was playing in Toronto, the terrible news was sent. He had been eliminated in the first round and didn't feel like taking Lundgren's calls. But Lundgren kept trying – it must be important. When Federer finally picked up, he learned that Carter had died in a car accident near the Kruger National Park in South Africa. His wife Silvia, who had been in a different car, had survived. Federer had recommended South Africa to Carter for his honeymoon and was devastated to hear of the tragedy. He ran through Toronto and back to his hotel in tears. It was the first time he had been confronted with death. A few days later he travelled on to Cincinnati, but his head was elsewhere. After the next 1st-round defeat, he returned to Basel on his 21st birthday to attend the funeral. "When I left the church, I was sadder than I had ever been in my life," he said. "Compared to that, a tennis defeat is nothing. There are so many things I would have wanted to say to him."

Federer needed time to fully recommit to tennis. During the indoor season he found his way back to his game, qualifying for the 2002 season finale of the top eight in Shanghai. The following year became his most successful year yet with the Wimbledon title and his outstanding triumph at the ATP Finals in Houston. His career was progressing well, but on the 9th of December 2003, Federer surprised the world by announcing his separation from Lundgren. Up to that point the two had seemed the perfect picture of a well-oiled team, but Federer now said that for him, the chemistry had been off for a while. He later described how the Wimbledon victory had changed the dynamics between them. All of a sudden it was no longer he who looked up to Lundgren, but the other way around. Again, his sense of purpose in pursuing his career was very clear.

At first, he continued without a coach and did very well. In 2004, he won Grand Slam titles two to four, reached number one for the first time and again dominated at the ATP Finals. Nonetheless, he continued looking for ways to improve – and hit upon Tony Roche. His interest in the 59-year-old was also linked to his soft spot for Australian tennis. The left-hander, once known for his excellent game at the net, was to spend a maximum of 15 weeks a year with him and help him develop his volleys. Federer no longer needed someone to explain tennis to him, but rather someone to help him polish details and discuss tactical subtleties.

Roche, a man of the old guard, also set new standards in training, driving him across the court for hours. In 2016, Federer described it in Wimbledon: "When Tony asked me, can you play seven times five sets? I looked at him, I go, 'I don't know.' He said, 'You want to be able to answer that question: yes, with no problem.' That's what I've worked for. Ever since then, I'm confident I can do it." The partnership was extremely successful. In 2005 and 2006, Federer played two excellent seasons with his best win-loss records ever – 81-4 and 92-5. Together with Roche he won six of nine possible major titles. He only missed out on a victory at the French Open, the only Grand Slam tournament in which his coach had won the Singles (1966). Two weeks before Roland Garros 2007, he separated from the Australian.

"The communication was bad. We weren't moving on," he explained. "Tony has to accept the decision, it's my career." Later he elaborated: "I couldn't feel his wholehearted commitment any more. I didn't feel that the fire was there. And I didn't want to have that as a distraction before the French Open, which was my big goal." This explanation again shows Federer's way of thinking: if he does something, it's 100%. Half-heartedness horrifies him.

Before Roland Garros, Davis Cup captain Severin Lüthi came on board – the coach from Bern became a constant in Federer's team. Lüthi had himself been a successful junior player; at the Orange Bowl in Miami, the unofficial junior world championships, he had beaten the later three-time French Open champion Gustavo Kuerten. But at 20, he accepted that he would never quite make it to the top and began an economics degree. At first, Lüthi was a helping hand, booking courts and organising practice partners, but he became ever more important for Federer. The passionate ice hockey fan (SC Bern) is smart and analytical, and has a keen sense of what Federer needs.

Failing again at the French Open in 2007, Federer brought in the experience of José Higueras for the 2008 clay court season. The Spaniard was an expert in slow surfaces, both as a player and coach, and had led Michael Chang (1989) and Jim Courier (1991) to victories in Paris. But he couldn't manage it with Federer, who even suffered his worst defeat against Rafael Nadal: he only won four games. Higueras stayed on until the US Open, which Federer won – a conciliatory end.

After the difficult year in which he lost the Wimbledon title, 2008, Federer enjoyed the golden summer of 2009 with the French/Wimbledon double and his first Grand Slam title as a father at the 2010 Australian Open. It was already his 16th. He nevertheless felt the need to develop his game. He realised that his dominance at the baseline was flagging – and not just against Nadal. So, in the late summer of 2010, he joined forces with Paul Annacone before the US Open. As a player, the American tended to "camp out at the net"; and as a coach, he had led Pete Sampras to 9 of his 14 major titles between 1995 and 2002. He was tasked with helping Federer return to a more offensive style. Looking back, Annacone explained what this meant: "Roger saw the new Rafa [Nadal], the new Andy [Murray], the new Novak [Djoković] playing so well. One of his biggest strengths is knowing himself. He understands what he can and can't do. And Roger is very pragmatic. He doesn't get emotional about the big decisions. That's allowed him to get better even as he's gotten older. It was about understanding how he could use his backhand to become more offensive even if it didn't seem offensive. Just certain patterns that would create discomfort to his opponents. And certain patterns that would create more opportunities to hit big forehands and finish at the net."

As ambitious and successful as Sampras and Federer both were, Annacone experienced how differently the two greats worked. Sampras demanded that Annacone give him his message in two to three minutes. Federer, by contrast, liked to discuss tactical subtleties in detail, question things, watch videos. Annacone calls him "the intellectual among the champions". His curiosity helps him to keep on developing at what is a relatively high age for professional tennis. Annacone didn't revolutionise him, instead beginning an evolution which continued under his successor **52** Stefan Edberg. The highlight of their collaboration was the Wimbledon victory in 2012. In October 2013, Federer and Annacone parted ways after a disappointing season riddled with injuries.

Federer immediately picked up the phone and called Stefan Edberg. Along with Becker and Sampras, the six-time Grand Slam champion had been one his childhood idols, winning three times on Federer's doorstep in Basel. Edberg was surprised by Federer's call. They had met in person the year before at the Stockholm Open and had had a friendly exchange, but the Swede had only been following professional tennis from a distance. He worked in finance, and his only tennis appearance was as his son's coach. Had it been anyone else, he would have declined, he told Göteborgs-Posten. But when Federer asks, you cannot say no. Edberg was not to be a classical coach. Lüthi stayed the main coach, whilst the Swede served to inspire and supply ideas. Federer described it as almost surreal to sit across from someone he had admired so much, debating tennis. He had probably thought: why not combine business with pleasure? Ironically, Edberg's former rival Becker also returned to professional tennis at almost exactly the same time – as Novak Djoković's coach.

Edberg's signature as one of the greatest net players in the sport was quickly visible in Federer's game. It seemed as though the younger wanted to prove to his elder that he, too, could play well at the net. Edberg taught him that the way you move to the net is just as important as the volley itself. Federer not only found a more aggressive style, but also revived his joy in the game. The partnership would have deserved a Grand Slam title – or two or three. Federer was playing better than he had in years, better even than during his last Wimbledon victory of 2012. But Djoković, of all people, coached by Becker, stole the show in the finals against him in Wimbledon (2014, 2015) and New York (2015). It seemed less of a technical than a mental problem: against Djoković, Federer seemed constrained and struggled to succeed with his aggressive game.

Edberg stayed in Federer's team for two years before being replaced by Croatian Ivan Ljubičić, former coach to Milos Raonic, in 2015. The separation was as friendly as can be, and from time to time, the Swede reappeared in Federer's box at Grand Slam tournaments. He likely wanted to see his seeds take root and his former mentee win major titles in person – as he had predicted. But Edberg and Ljubičić had a long wait. When drawing a bath for his daughters after the Australian Open in 2016, Federer's left knee made a cracking sound. Though it felt harmless at first, it meant meniscal surgery. Federer faced an operation for the first time in his life. And although the procedure was successful and Federer enjoyed a comeback after a good two months, his left knee never fully recovered, and, thanks to uneven weight distribution, his back issues flared up again. After Wimbledon, Federer pulled the emergency brakes and sat out the rest of the 2016 season. But he stuck with Ljubičić. The 6 ft 4 in man who had himself played against him and even beaten him 3 times (in 15 matches) was not just a suitable coach, but also occasional sparring **54** partner, still in good shape and with an excellent serve.

Without question, Ljubičić continued in Edberg's spirit. After all, he himself had picked up the racket out of admiration for the Swede. Ljubičić's life story is a touching one. At 13, the war in Yugoslavia forced him to leave his hometown of Banja Luka in today's Bosnia-Herzegovina with his mother and three-year-old brother. He became a pro thanks to a tennis camp in Turin, where he made an impression. Another plus for Ljubičić was that he had himself played against Federer's rivals and knew from experience how Nadal's extreme topspin shots and the gruelling rallies against Djoković felt. He had his finger on the pulse. Federer and Ljubičić's patience paid off: at the Australian Open 2017, they celebrated the tennis virtuoso's first Grand Slam title in four and a half years. And that opened the floodgates to further successes. In Wimbledon 2017 and Melbourne 2018, Federer also emerged victorious, watched in Australia, as always, by Diana and Bob Carter, Peter's parents.

At their son's funeral in 2002, they met the Federer of whom their son had spoken so often for the second time. Since then they had kept in regular contact. On the sidelines of the Davis Cup semi-finals in 2003 in Melbourne, the Carters had their first longer exchange with Federer. "That Davis Cup weekend was very, very emotional because it was when we really got to know Roger," Bob Carter told The Australian, a Sydney daily, in 2012. "He took us into an empty room, on our own, and we had a really good and long talk. That's where he got to know us, too. We told him... we said to him, Roger, just do the best you can, mate. Peter always thought the world of you." The relationship with Federer helped the Carters to come to terms with the loss of their son. Since 2005, Federer invites them to the Australian Open, covering all the expenses. Whilst in the beginning they stayed for the whole two weeks, it eventually became a bit much. Nowadays they only come for the final. Which recently has tended to pay off.

"He wasn't my first coach, but he was my real coach," Federer highlights Carter's influence. "Thanks to him I have my entire technique and coolness. He knew me and my game and he always knew what was good for me." Federer once even said that Carter is always with him on the court. An interview with CNN in early 2019 shows that this is more than an empty phrase. The interviewer asks Federer: "He [Carter] passed away the year before you won your first slam at Wimbledon, obviously. What do you think he would have thought to see you here now with 20 Grand Slams?" Federer pauses briefly, then breaks down in tears. "Sorry. Oh, man, I still miss him so much. I hope he would be proud," he says. "I guess he didn't want me to be a wasted talent."

It's that special connection which makes Carter's parents' presence at his victories so important to Federer. The feeling is mutual. Diana and Bob Carter follow his career with pride – almost as if he were their son.

6. Mirka, the goldsmith

First impressions don't always count. Thankfully. Otherwise the dream team of Swiss tennis, Miroslava Vavrinec
and Roger Federer, would never have existed. Nor, in its
current form, would the stellar career in which Federer's
wife had a key part to play; her first impression of teenage Federer was not a good one. Mirka, as everyone calls
her, saw him for the first time in his youth, when he played
for Tennis Club Old Boys Basel. "I was playing club tennis
in Switzerland and everybody said, 'Go see this guy, he's
super talented, the future of tennis'," he told The Guard-
ian in a personal interview in 2016. "And the first thing she
saw was me throwing a racket and shouting, and she was
like [mockingly], 'Yeah! Great player, he seems really good!
What's wrong with this guy?'" But Federer had a second
chance and showed another side to himself – witty, sensitive, smitten.

The 2000 Summer Olympics in Sydney were ill-fated
for Swiss Tennis: the star players Martina Hingis, Patty
Schnyder and Marc Rosset had all withdrawn. So the small
tennis delegation made up of young Federer, Vavrinec, Em-
manuelle Gagliardi and their coach Peter Lundgren shared

a house in the Olympic Village with four Swiss wrestlers. Nobody had even an inkling of the romance which was to blossom under the Australian sun. Even before the Games, Vavrinec told Swiss journalists that Federer had given her a stomach ache by making her laugh so much. She liked that he wasn't a bore, but rather a joker who always put everyone in a good mood. But for a long time, she didn't realise that he was interested in her: "I just didn't get why he wanted to talk to me so much," she said later.

On the court, Federer missed two chances at a medal: in the semi-finals against Tommy Haas and in the bronze medal match against Arnaud di Pasquale. But off court he took his shot: on the last day, he summoned all his courage and kissed Mirka. She liked it, but joked: "You're still so young. A baby." He had just turned 19, she was already 22. "She's a little older than me, and women mature earlier anyway. That helped me a lot when we got together," he says in hindsight. "Our relationship quickly got very serious."

Initially, the two were able to keep their romance from the public eye. Even though it was an open secret in the tennis scene in the summer of 2001, at Federer's request it only became public during the US Open. By then it was also nearly impossible to hide, given that they both eagerly watched each other's matches from the stands and that Federer's coach, Peter Lundgren, was also working with Vavrinec. "The cool kid from Basel and the beauty from Thurgau – they share more than net cord, aces and break points. The two play ball off-court, too," revealed the Zurich tabloid SonntagsBlick. The reporter let his imagination run wild: "She kisses him when he wins, which is often. He comforts her when she loses, which is not so rare. For months now, Roger and Mirka have been making their way through the daily jealousy, resentment and relentless competition of the hectic professional tour together." Vavrinec offers a quote, saying: "It's not easy. Thank God there's phones and texting. Because we only play together at Grand Slam tournaments and in Key Biscayne."

It soon became easier – albeit unintentionally. In New York, Vavrinec enjoyed her best result yet, the third round in a Grand Slam tournament. And in early 2002, she appeared at the popular team competition, the Hopman Cup in Perth, to play at Federer's side. But in the early months of that year, chronic foot problems force her to retire from professional tennis. She played her last match on the tour two weeks after her 24th birthday. In her short career, she made it to 76th in the world and played her way to USD 260,832 in prize money.

Vavrinec was born on the 1st of April 1978 in Bojnice, Slovakia, and raised in Kreuzlingen in the Canton of Thurgau. Her parents Miroslav and Drahomira had fled to Switzerland with their only child when she was two. Her father is a goldsmith and for years ran a jewellery shop in the Karussell shopping centre in Kreuzlingen. To this day, her father offers his services as a goldsmith online. It was his passion for sports which rubbed off on his daughter. In 1987, he took her to a tennis tournament in nearby Filderstadt in Germany. There, nine-year-old Mirka met her idol Martina Navratilova and handed her a pair of earrings which her father had made. Navratilova was enchanted, telling her young fan that she had the athletic build for the sport, and put her in touch with her fellow countryman Jiří Granat, who had settled in Switzerland.

The former top 100 player, who had often played mixed doubles with Navratilova as a junior, offered Vavrinec a trial class and, although she hadn't been playing long, saw something special. "She was very flexible and agile," says Granat. "But what I particularly noticed: she really wanted it. Lots of children play tennis because it's what their parents want. She had her own drive, she wanted to learn something." Granat coached Vavrinec a few times, but since her family lived in Kreuzlingen, an hour away, it never developed into a long-term collaboration. But a few years later, when Vavrinec was getting ready to compete at international juniors' tournaments, her parents got in touch again – and Granat accompanied the 17-year-old to the junior competitions at Roland Garros and Wimbledon as her coach. Next to her enormous will and work ethic, what he particularly remembers from that time is her independence: "She was much more autonomous than the other juniors I had met through Swiss Tennis. Most of them relied far too much on their parents. They practically carried their bags onto the court for them. Mirka was completely different – she organised everything herself. Even for her mother, who was usually with her at tournaments. It was more Mirka organising things for her mother than the other way round." Today, still, her organisational skills are in high demand, more than ever, in fact, as the head of the "Delegation Federer" which together with four children, nannies, private tutor and coaches comprises more than ten people.

Vavrinec's career was over before it had even really begun. But she had gathered valuable experiences which were to prove useful for the best male player's career path. "The fact that she played professionally is a huge advantage for Roger," Granat is convinced. "She understands every situation. She knows how he feels when he's won. She knows how to speak to him when he's lost. It's hard to put yourself in those shoes if you haven't experienced it yourself. She knows what to react to, and what to let lie. And what he needs to be able to concentrate on his tennis." Because to succeed in this sport, you need to be free to be selfish. Not all the time, but at certain points, for instance during a Grand Slam tournament. There's no space for compromise there. You can't waste valuable energy, recovery and preparation come first. Players who get up three times in the night to change nappies or comfort children don't win finals the next day.

It wasn't a conscious choice to date a fellow player, Federer tells The New York Times in 2012. "But in my situation, I think it really does help, because she knows in some ways what it takes, and she did it on a level that was still very good but not at my level. And she already put in a massive amount of hours herself. So when I tell her, 'Look, I need to go to practice,' she's the first to say, 'I know, I know you need it.'" Marc Rosset, the Genevan Olympic champion of 1992 and one of those who introduced Federer to the ATP

Tour, said: "Half of his success is Mirka's. They say behind every great man is a strong woman. That's true of Federer. Mirka has always lightened the load. She has his back, so that he can concentrate on tennis. He's collected so many titles and so much money on the side. When he injured his knee [in February 2016] she could have said: 'It's not so bad, you've already achieved so much.' But she encouraged him to go on."

62   Her relationship with Federer helped Vavrinec to come to terms with the end of her own career. After her withdrawal from the tour in 2000, her life continued almost seamlessly – in a different role. With Federer she could enjoy what she herself had been denied as an athlete. During Wimbledon 2004, she told the Zurich-based Tages-Anzeiger: "When Roger wins, it's as if I were winning too. I feel it so intensely and I know what it means. He shares everything with me. On some level, Roger gives me back my tennis life. I enjoy being back on tour. And now everything is even more intense than in the time when I played myself, since he's number one." These words are quoted often as they come from the last longer personal interview she gave. Whilst in the early days she also worked as Federer's press manager and had to send a lot of refusals, she later passed the task on to his manager, Tony Godsick, and stopped speaking publicly. Not least on Federer's recommendation, careful as he is about what his immediate circle say in public. His wife isn't on Twitter, Facebook, Instagram or Snapchat. Just an unofficial fan page on Instagram, with 62,000 followers – and counting.

The fact that she hasn't given any interviews in 10 years gives her an air of mystery. But she reveals much of herself just through her appearances in Federer's box during his matches. How in great matches she suffers, too, folding or throwing up her hands, cheering and fuming. During the dramatic Swiss semi-final of the 2014 ATP Finals in London, Federer's opponent Stan Wawrinka complained that her interjections were distracting him. When, in a critical moment of the decisive third set, he told her off, she shouted "Cry baby!" at him. A no-go in the gentlemen's sport of tennis. An irritated Wawrinka lost the match after four missed match points, in the changing rooms the two Swiss players had a heated exchange. But a week later, they pulled themselves together and won the Davis Cup – beating France in the final in Lille.

There's another episode which shows how passionately Mirka follows her husband's matches – although this one wasn't caught on microphone. According to American journalist Jon Wertheim's book "Strokes of Genius", she supposedly caught him front of the locker rooms after the first rain break of the 2008 Wimbledon final against Rafael Nadal. She reminded him who was the five-time champion. He listened in silence and nodded meekly. The pep talk worked, he returned to the court as if transformed and returned from being 0-2 down – before losing the fifth set.

"She was a big believer in me not wasting any sort of talent," says Federer. "Because she knew herself that she was limited to a degree. She was extremely hardworking, but she knew with my talents I could achieve so many more

»Whether he wants to or not, Federer shapes other people's lives. Their admiration for him at times borders on the religious.«

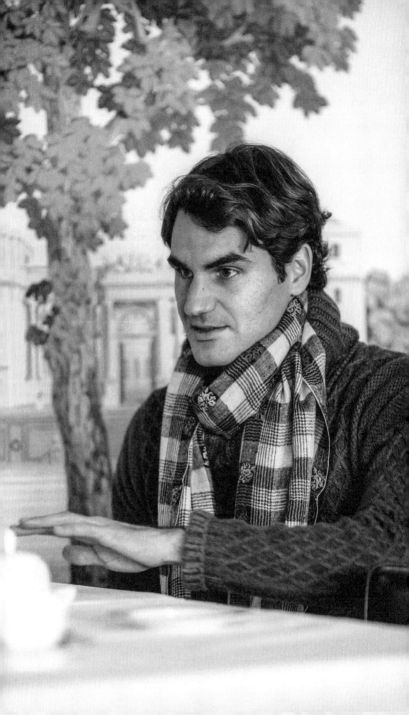

things." And although from 2009 her priority shifted to motherhood, even after the birth of the twin girls, Myla and Charlene, her influence on sporting questions is not to be underestimated. In 2012, Federer's coach at the time, Paul Annacone, told the New York Times: "She still plays a huge role and has great input and impact. She understands the big picture extremely well and does a great job in terms of letting us work but also shares invaluable information. This is a tricky balance. She's been there since day one, so she knows very well what it takes and how to get there." And she's not one to shy away from telling her husband what she thinks to his face. Even if it hurts.

"She's been a rock in my corner," Federer often says of Mirka. If it weren't for her wholehearted participation in his career, he would long have hung up the tennis racket. He's stressed that often. In Wimbledon 2017, he didn't mince his words: "Without her I couldn't do it. If she said, you know, I don't want to travel no more, I'll say, okay, my career is over. It's as simple as that. (...) I'm happy she allows me to chase our dreams really, because she's in it as much as I am." And after the triumph at the 2018 Australian Open he emphasised: "Without her support, I wouldn't be playing tennis anymore since many years. But we had a very open conversation, if she was happy to do this or not, years ago. I'm happy that she's super supportive, and she's willing to take on a massive workload with the kiddies. Same for me, because I wouldn't want to be away from my kids for more than two weeks. This life wouldn't work if she said no."

Everything has become more complicated since the pair

became parents. Myla and Charlene were born on the 23rd of July 2009, the twin sons Leo and Lennart on the 6th of May 2014. After their daughters' birth, the British bookmakers Ladbrokes offered odds of 100/1 that one of the two would win Wimbledon one day. And 200/1 for them to do it together in the doubles. Their sons however show a greater interest in tennis. Nowadays, a coach nurtures the children's sporting abilities when travelling.

Although the logistics of travelling with the big family and their whole entourage are complicated, Federer only very rarely flies to tournaments alone – for instance to Shanghai, his only autumn event of the Asian tour. When asked before the 2018 Australian Open which phase of his career he had enjoyed the most, he said: "Now is unbelievable. In my vision I never had this, that I was going to be playing tennis with four kids. The dominance. Of course, it's fun winning. But it was very stressful. One week here, one week there. Another award here, another practice there. It was never ending. And family was something I always wanted once I got together with Mirka. My life changed completely. It's the best thing that has ever happened to me. This phase, the last eight years have been the best. I am a big family man."

Although Vavrinec played a central role in the Federer success story, she isn't universally liked in Switzerland. Perhaps because she left room for interpretation, not having spoken publicly for so long. Her texting during matches or her (bold) pink Gucci jumper with a roaring tiger on, spotted it wearing in the stands at the 2017 Australian Open, made her quite the subject of conversation in the little Alpine nation. In the case of the jumper, the discussion was less about her fashion taste but rather how much the famous piece cost (around USD 1,500). Which of course says more about the pettiness of many Swiss people than it does about her.

At any rate, no perception of her could be more wrong than that of a woman who's made herself comfortable and simply benefits from her husband's success. She has many roles to play: those of partner, mother, motivator, comforter, cook, organiser, adviser, the first supporter – and many more. Although she never learned her father's craft, she can safely be called a goldsmith.

7. Federer and the four seasons of tennis

Melbourne, Paris, London, New York – part of the allure of professional tennis is its four seasons. When, in the first few months of the year, there's still snow outside in our climes, the tennis whizzes and their sizzling battles in Melbourne bring a little summer into our living rooms. In June, when every self-respecting hobby player is staining his socks red on the court, the clay king is crowned at Roland Garros. In Wimbledon, the lily-white costumes are a celebration of lawn tennis, the most original form of the sport. And in September, the best and most perseverant battle it out long into the night under the light of the New York floodlights – invoking Frank Sinatra's line: "If I can make it there, I'll make it anywhere."

Each of the four Grand Slam tournaments has its own character and its own particular charm. Roger Federer dubbed the Australian Open the "Happy Slam", because everyone there is so relaxed. Paris loves players with a certain flair, the French, and sometimes those who win. Every corner of the All England Club sparkles with carefully curated tennis history. And nowhere is as loud as Flushing Meadows, where the sport is staged as a show, film stars and musicians wave and make faces to the crowds on the big screen, and the airplanes from nearby LaGuardia Airport roar over the complex. Melbourne smells of coconut sun cream, Paris of Chanel No. 5 and crêpes, Wimbledon of strawberries and freshly mowed grass, and New York of the big, wide world.

When a young Roger spent hours playing ball after ball against the garage door, he dreamed of winning Wimbledon and raising the golden trophy with the little pineapple on the lid up in the air. Although he grew up as a clay court player, his heroes were the champions of the holy lawns at Church Road – first Boris Becker, then Stefan Edberg and finally, Pete Sampras. It felt fascinatingly exotic, exclusive, unattainable. "I only knew lawns from my own garden and from football," he says, looking back. "I always felt it must be something dignified – because only the best are allowed to play on grass." There were no public grass courts in Switzerland at the time. Federer had to wait until he was 16 to play on grass for the first time at a junior invitational tournament at Queen's Club, London, in the summer of 1998. He lost in the second round, but quickly warmed to the unfamiliar ground. It's practically made for his light-footedness, his attacking style and his deep backhand slice.

A few weeks after his grass court debut, he took part in the juniors' tournament at Wimbledon and was so nervous before his first match that he thought the net was too high. But it wasn't, and he charged to the title without losing a set. He had to skip the Champions' Dinner, having to go straight on to Gstaad, where he had been given a wildcard for his debut on the ATP Tour. He was to have plenty more chances to take part in the victory gala in London. No other tournament has defined his career like Wimbledon. It was there that at 19, he toppled his idol Sampras in the fourth round – their only encounter on the pro tour. It was there that in 2003, he celebrated his first Grand Slam title, there that in 2009, his 15th broke Sampras' previous record. There that he suffered his most bitter defeat against arch-rival Rafael Nadal in 2008. And there that, with eight titles, he holds the record for its entire 150-year history.

But his significance for the tournament – and vice-versa – extends beyond the sport itself. Where Sampras was admired for his cool efficiency, Federer is loved for his virtuosity, joyful play and grace. His symbiosis of classical play and modern execution are a perfect fit for the All England Club, which carefully curates its traditions, but is also undergoing a rapid change. Federer's greatest achievements are not his eight Wimbledon titles, quips English journalist Mark Hodgkinson, who has written several books about him (including "Fedegraphica" and "Federesque"). But rather that he has succeeded in getting the reserved, buttoned-up Brits to abandon their reserve – at least for the two or three hours during which he floats across the lawn. After Federer's eighth title at Church Road, Hodgkinson wrote in a column for the Swiss SonntagsZeitung: "Yes, a few London schoolgirls fainted over Björn Borg in the 1970s, but this is a whole different level of fandom. If Borg was a rock star of the lawns, Federer is regarded as an icon, a statesman, the alpha male of that green and purple world. Grown men in their 40s, 50s, 60s or even older are the ones leading this;

they tend to be the Fed Heads in chief." Hodgkinson doubts the English have ever loved a tennis player as they love him. It was striking that almost nobody resented Federer when, in 2012, he beat Andy Murray in the final and reduced him to tears – extending Britain's 76-year wait for a home victory by yet another year.

Wimbledon's class and tradition also left its mark on Federer. The boy who just loved to play tennis became a gentleman of the courts. One who usually does and says the right thing. Chairman Tim Phillips didn't have to think long about who to seat next to Queen Elizabeth II at lunch in the clubhouse when, after 33 years, she finally visited again on the 24th of June 2010: Federer, of course. He proved an entertaining but unobtrusive conversationalist, as hoped. But, says Phillips, it speaks to his character that Federer treats everyday members of staff with the same respect as he does the Queen. Wimbledon and Federer are made for one another. Even after 20 years, the tournament holds the same allure for him as the very first time. When he shared his walk through the empty grounds before the beginning of the 2018 tournament on Instagram Live, he seemed like a child in a sweetshop. He ambled past Court 18, the site of the 11-hour-long record epic between John Isner and Nicholas Mahut ("still my favourite match") and at Henman Hill smiled mischievously and asked: "Where's Tim hiding?"

Were Federer to rank Grand Slams by his own order of preference, the Australian Open would be second. He came into contact with Australia early on – on being introduced to the Australian coach, Peter Carter, in the Tennis Club Old Boys Basel aged nine. Carter raved about the legends of his home country, about Rod Laver, Roy Emerson, Ken Rosewall or John Newcombe, and taught him a classical Australian style of play. Later, Federer was also coached by Tony Roche (2005 – 2007). Australians therefore feel part of Federer's success, particularly since he cultivates a style of tennis which reminds them of their former greats. A 2016 study of the Australian sports marketing company Gemba Group found him to be the most popular athlete in Australia – ahead of any locals. **73**

Critical moments of his life, both private and professional, played out Down Under: he first kissed Mirka Vavrinec during the 2000 Olympic Games in Sydney. In 2003, he lost the critical fourth rubber against Lleyton Hewitt in the Davis Cup semi-finals in Melbourne after a two-set lead – a painful defeat which spurred him on. In 2004, he reached number one at the Australian Open for the first time, after winning the semi-final against Juan Carlos Ferrero (naturally, he also won the title). During the 2006 award ceremony, he first met Rod Laver and was so overwhelmed that he burst into tears. In 2010, he won his first Grand Slam title as a father at the Yarra River; in 2017, he launched his astonishing comeback at the same spot. By now, six titles make the Australian Open his second-best Grand Slam tournament. He likes the ease, the sportsmanship and passion for sports of Australia. And he finds it infectious, even developing an affinity for the Australian national sport: cricket. "To me, Australia is a way of life," he says. "That's why the country will always be something like a second home to me." It was love at first sight.

The same can't be said for New York. The hubbub of the Big Apple was initially too much for him. And so on his first five tries, he never got further than the round of 16. But once he opened himself up to the buzzing metropolis, he was unstoppable. From 2004 to 2008, he won five times in a row – something no one in the open era (since **74** 1968) had succeeded in doing. And victory is the best way to win over an American audience. Once they had accepted that the Americans were no longer winning, they swung round to Federer. "If there's one thing that New Yorkers love, then it's whoever or whatever is the best," says Chris Widmaier, Managing Director of Corporate Communications for the United States Tennis Association (USTA). And, he adds, when Federer appears in adverts with the golfer Tiger Woods and the (former) baseball player Derek Jeter, most people no longer even realised that they were seeing two Americans and a European.

Federer's winning streak at the US Open was also an important building block for marketing purposes. Because unlike the stars of the four big professional leagues (baseball, basketball, American football and ice hockey), who are constantly on American television, he only plays in America for a few weeks each year. His connection with Vogue editor-in-chief Anna Wintour, portrayed as a ruthless boss in the film "The Devil Wears Prada", makes him even more famous in the United States. The trendsetter with a famous bob first met Federer at a lunch in 2005 and promptly fell for him (or rather his tennis). She includes him in the legendary fashion magazine more often than any other athlete and travels the world to see him live. "Everyone calls themself a Roger Federer fan," she wrote in a column in autumn 2017. "I consider myself a groupie." She wants to talk to him about tennis, he wants to talk fashion – and more often than not he gains the upper hand. It's evident that Wintour has an enormous influence on both his wardrobe and that of his wife Mirka.

When it comes to his relationship status with Roland Garros, Federer would probably have to click: "It's complicated." He dropped the whole clay court seasons in 2017 and 2018, even though he was in good health. When it comes to his priorities, Paris clearly suffers at the hands of Wimbledon. Federer has little time for Mats Wilander's suggestion that he could just practise on clay for a few days and then just play the French Open without too many expectations. "I don't just play along a bit. I have higher standards." That's understandable. After all, for years he was the second-best clay court player in the world.

But at Roland Garros, Nadal was his undoing, time and time again. Until 2009, when the clay court king, who ruled with an iron fist, was toppled completely unexpectedly after 33 successive match wins in Paris – in the fourth round by Swedish giant Robin Söderling. Faced with the unique opportunity which now presented itself, Federer's hands began to tremble. Against Tommy Haas (round of 16), he found himself down two sets to love, against Juan Martin Del Potro in the semi-finals he was led two sets to one. In the final against Söderling he regained his grip and completed his Grand Slam collection. In the second week, the Parisian crowds effectively carried him to the title. "Allez Roger" sounded from all sides. The fashion capital has a soft spot for him not just because of his elegance, but also because, thanks to his training in French-speaking Switzerland, he speaks the language almost perfectly. But is there really anywhere he isn't readily adopted?

8. Fred Astaire vs. Rambo – the rivalry with Nadal

Rivalry is the icing on the sporting cake. It's often what really makes athletes into tangible people, pushing them to their limits and distinguishing them. What would Muhammad Ali have been without Joe Frazier? John McEnroe without Björn Borg? Ayrton Senna without Alain Prost? Carl Lewis without Ben Johnson? Martina Navratilova without Chris Evert? Magic Johnson without Larry Bird? Greg LeMond without Laurent Fignon? And who would Roger Federer be without Rafael Nadal? Perhaps a 30-time major champion. After all, he lost nine Grand Slam encounters with his fiercest rival, six of them finals: 2006, 2007, 2008 and 2011 at the French Open, Wimbledon 2008 and at the 2009 Australian Open.

Although these defeats hurt Federer and his fans, it was good that in Nadal, he had the most uncomfortable opponent conceivable: in his years of dominance and brilliance, where victory was almost taken for granted, it drew out his fighting spirit. Nadal drove him to improve ever further, even to reinvent himself. Borg yielded aged 25 after finding his master in McEnroe. After the 1981 US Open, the third Grand Slam final lost to the American, three years his junior, he had had enough. Federer was undaunted by Nadal. One might even hazard the theory that Federer's true greatness was only revealed when he started to lose more often. Next to many successful records, he also holds one of a different kind: no one in the hundred-year history of tennis has lost as many Grand Slam finals against the same rival as he has – six defeats against Nadal.

The rivalry between the two is fascinating in part due to the athletic quality and explosiveness of their encounters, but also lives off the contrast between them: grace against force, the ballet dancer against the boxer, the emperor of the grass against the king of clay, the righty against the lefty, classical technique against the cutting-edge, the dandy against the pirate, the ambassador for Mercedes against one for Kia, the cool central European against the fiery Southerner.

You might dare an artistic comparison: where Federer evokes an impressionist like Pierre-Auguste Renoir with his fine brushstrokes, Nadal is the wild Van Gogh. Each is a genius in his own way. Whilst Federer radiates a calm confidence, his emotions under control, Nadal is bubbling with energy, intensity and passion. When, after two hours, Federer's shirt still seems bone dry, his rival has already soaked three. After the Wimbledon final in 2007, in which Federer barely defended his territory against Nadal's attack, the Times of London spoke of a battle between Fred Astaire and Rambo. It hardly needs saying that Federer is the legendary tap-dancer.

Sportswear giant Nike has had both of the exceptional

players on its roster for a long time and played to their differences in their outfits and advertising. Where Nadal appeared in sleeveless shirts which emphasise his imposing biceps and contribute to his pirate image, Federer strode across the court at Wimbledon in white jackets and even with a gentleman's handbag. Federer or Nadal, the question is driving tennis aficionados around the world for over a decade. You can like and admire both, but you have to choose. Or do you know any tennis fans who really root for **79** both to win? Well, there you go. Federer or Nadal – it's a matter of conscience.

Their rivalry began on the 29th of March 2004 with a bombshell in Miami. Having reached number one for the first time after the Australian Open, Federer seemed to have left the competition behind him. In the first few months of the year, he had won 23 of 24 matches before facing the Spanish teenager for the first time in the second round – and at 3-6, 3-6, didn't stand a chance. He was still a little weakened by the sunstroke which had hit him the week before in Indian Wells. Nonetheless, Miami was a taste of what he had in store from Nadal in the coming years. The disappointed favourite later said he hadn't been able to properly implement his attacking game. And wondered: "He doesn't hit the ball flat and hard. It's more with a lot of spin, which makes the ball bounce, bounce high, and that's a struggle I had today. I tried to get out of it, but kind of couldn't." A journalist asked cheekily: "As the world No. 1, still only 22, does it frighten you that he is almost five years younger than you?" Federer had to admit that Nadal was indeed very mature for his age. But it was one thing to join the tour as a newcomer with nothing to lose, and another to prove your mettle afterwards. "I think he's enjoying his tennis. That's exactly what he should do. We'll see how strong he will be in two years."

Stronger than Federer would like. His Mallorcan rival missed the 2004 French Open due to a stress fracture in his ankle, but a year later he celebrated his first Grand Slam title in Paris two days after his 19th birthday, on which he beat Federer in four sets in the semi-final. From 2006 to 2008, the two faced off in 13 finals, with summits in their respective kingdoms – Paris and Wimbledon. At Roland Garros, Nadal proved himself the clay court king, and in 2008, even toppled the Swiss ruler from his throne at the All England Club in a final for the history books.

At the time, Federer was pursuing his sixth successive Wimbledon title, with which he would beat Björn Borg's record (1976 – 1980). But the dressing-down from Nadal a month before (6–1, 6–3, 6–0) had left its mark. In Wimbledon, Federer lost the first two sets, towards the end of the third the rain forced an 80-minute break. It helped Federer. He won sets three and four and, in the fifth, saw his chance. But at the end of the road, Nadal was more determined and managed the decisive break to 8-7. Had they both held serve at 7-7, the match would have been postponed to Monday at 8-8. It was already 9.17 p.m., the ball hard to make out at grass level, when Federer's last forehand caught the net and Nadal fell to the ground.

American journalist Jon Wertheim (Sports Illustrated)

dedicated the worthwhile book "Strokes of Genius" to the epic match, and in the summer of 2018, the Tennis Channel brought out a two-hour documentary of the same name. Was that final really the greatest tennis match of all time? It's doubtful whether it was the best tennis they have ever played against each other. Federer was not at his best and in that final only discovered his fighting spirit when he seemed hopelessly behind. But the drama of the match, a battle of the greats over 4 hours and 48 minutes, is almost **81** unsurpassable.

The Frenchman Richard Gasquet, who had had the pleasure of playing both of them frequently – against Federer, he is 2-17, against Nadal 0-16 –, puts their respective strengths in a nutshell. He is quoted by Argentine tennis journalist Sebastián Fest in his book about the Federer-Nadal rivalry ("The Lives and Careers of Two Tennis Legends") as follows: "The two of them are very different. Federer's ball is fast, he leaves you no time to breathe, hits it the instant it bounces, and gains fractions of a second that make everything harder for his rival. Nadal's ball, on the other hand, is very heavy. You see it coming and it throws you back. You have to be deeply entrenched in order to hold up against it and return it well. There's no one else who hits it like that."

Federer, too, has trouble with Nadal's extreme forehand strokes – the ball spins around 50 to 80 times a second. To understand why he has struggled so much (and for so long) against the Spaniard, let's remember good old Achilles. The mythical Greek hero was invincible because his mother, the sea nymph Thetis, had dipped him in the River Styx. However, as she held him by the foot when doing it, he had a weak spot there which stayed vulnerable: his Achilles' heel. Federer's Achilles' heel is the one-handed backhand, and nobody can attack it as precisely as Nadal with his powerful left-handed forehand.

Complicated though these matches became for Federer, they were simple for Nadal, as he describes in his entertaining 2011 autobiography "Rafa": "If I have to hit the ball 20 times to Federer's backhand, I'll hit it 20 times, not 19. (...) Even if you see what seems like a chance to put the pressure on and seize the initiative, keep hitting to the backhand, because in the long run, over the course of the whole game, that is what's wisest and best. That's the plan. It's not a complicated plan. You can't even call it a tactic, it's so simple." And further: "With Federer, what you have to do is keep applying pressure to the backhand, make him play the ball high, strike with the racket up where his neck is, put him under pressure, wear him down. Probe chinks that way in his game and his morale. Frustrate him, drive him close to despair, if you can." Time and time again Nadal succeeds in doing just that. And in the stands, Uncle Toni enjoys the show. Because it was him who put the racket in the right-handed boy's left hand – to give Nadal an edge against the mostly right-handed competition. Nadal gets under Federer's skin. After his defeat in the Australian Open final in 2009, the disenchanted tennis king even broke out in tears during his post-match speech and was comforted by his Spanish conqueror.

Nadal is the ultimate challenge for Federer. As early as 2005, he began to train specifically for Nadal's game with fellow left-hander Tony Roche. But it was only in the golden autumn of his career that he cracked the puzzle. The long break in the second half of 2016 thanks to his knee injury helped. In 2017, he attacked Nadal with new vigour and a different strategy. He played far more aggressively with his backhand, thus reversing the dynamics between him and his rival. He came over his backhand on the return, rather than slicing the ball back like before, and rather than retreating during backhanded rallies, he stuck to the baseline, staying on the offense.

Tennis expert Heinz Günthardt explains: "This way, Nadal's spin has less power, and Federer can catch more momentum on the backhand. But of course it takes exceptional timing." In technical terms, Federer doesn't change anything, but with a new mentality and more dynamic leg work he turns his backhand weakness into a strength. And so, in the final of the 2017 Australian Open, his 11th Grand Slam match against Nadal, he won more than half the rallies in which the ball was played to his backhand for the very first time. In the fifth set, which Federer won 6-3 after being 1-3 down, he hit eight winners with his backhand alone. All of a sudden, Nadal's patented recipe against Federer stopped working. Australian tennis analyst Craig O'Shannessy says: "The backhand used to be Federer's weakness his opponents could target. Now they don't know where to play to anymore. It is as if he had two forehands." What a difference a small tactical shift can make!

Although so much is at stake between them and Federer and Nadal have spent years competing for tennis world dominance, they seem to get on well. Federer reached out to Nadal early on, who was initially shy off court and spoke very little English. In October 2005, Federer visited him in his hotel room in Basel for a chat before the tournament. Both were missing the Swiss Indoors due to injury, but Nadal had come to Basel anyway to meet tournament director Roger Brennwald. Federer and Nadal chatted about their injuries, about the season, and their plans for the upcoming months.

Such a relaxed meeting, even just for 20 minutes, would have been unimaginable between McEnroe and Connors or Agassi and Sampras – although they were fellow countrymen. And Ivan Lendl wasn't liked by anybody anyway. Someone like Connors, for whom tennis was more than just a game, still shakes his head over how well Federer and Nadal get on. Their good relationship is probably built on the fact that for all their differences on the court, they have a lot in common as people. Both are family men, grew up with similar values, prefer stability and reliability in their private lives. Nadal has been with his girlfriend Xisca Perelló since his youth, Federer with Mirka for more than 18 years. And in both cases, their parents are actively involved in their careers, but quickly left their tennis to the care of others.

The only time it got prickly between the two was after their epic five-hour final at the Foro Italico in Rome in 2006, after Federer had complained that Nadal was taking too much time between points. Nadal was offended and showed it. But although the issue has simmered over years and journalists do their very best to bring it to a boil, the conflict never escalated. Their respect for one another is too great. They also crossed one another in the Player Council, which Federer presided over for quite some time with Nadal as his deputy. Nadal accused Federer of not doing enough to reform the jam-packed tournament calendar and resigned in 2012. But most of the time, there's a tangible affection between them. Their attempt to record a short advert for the 2010 "Match for Africa" in Zurich is delightful. The script was pretty simple:

Federer "So Rafa, do you know what you're going to give me for Christmas yet?"
Nadal "You know what, I'm gonna come to Switzerland and play an exhibition match for your foundation."
Federer "That's very nice, thank you!"
Nadal "And what present are you gonna give me?"
Federer "I'll give you the first set, how's that?"
Nadal "That's nice."
Federer "Yeah, nice."
Nadal "So, see you in Zurich."

It took them 20 minutes to wrap. Because whenever Federer looked at Rafa, he just burst out laughing – infecting Rafa, too. The event in the Hallenstadion Zurich was a huge success, and the next day they played in Madrid for Nadal's foundation. They quickly realised how much they could achieve when they worked together. Thus in 2016, Federer was there at the opening of Nadal's tennis academy in Mallorca, helping to get it more publicity. It was almost moving when, in the first ever Laver Cup in September 2017, they first played on the same team and even doubles together. And when Federer won the decisive point for the Europeans in his last singles match, Nadal leaped on him. We'll just assume without any intention of hurting his injury-prone back.

After the Laver Cup, Federer described his relationship with Nadal as follows: "We had hard and painful battles on court, issues as well, but there was always an enormous respect between us. We shared many strong moments on court and off court in a very friendly way. As we grew up, I realised how important Rafa was in my career. He will forever be my ultimate opponent. He was the one who helped me improve the most and be a better player. And at the same time, I say that if he didn't exist, I would have not won so much. Rafa's presence was an extra motivation."

If this force of nature from Mallorca hadn't shown up and destroyed Federer's game with brute strength, the latter might not have become a 30-time Grand Slam champion, but rather retired far too early. After all, isn't it harder to appreciate the things which come easy? And it's the things we fight hardest for which drive us the furthest.

9. A modern classic

From time to time, Christophe Freyss likes to reward himself with a Federer match. Without interruptions. Or even just a set.

"It's a joy to see what he's become," says the 62-year-old Frenchman. "And it makes me proud, because I invested a lot of work in him. Roger shows everything you love about tennis. And it just looks so natural." Freyss was the national coach for Swiss Tennis when the promising talent from rural Basel was admitted to the national training programme (Tennis Etudes) in Ecublens. After the admission test, which included a test match, Freyss confirmed that the junior from Tennis Club Old Boys Basel had "natural talent, as well as basic technique without any major flaws," as reported in the Basler Zeitung. That doesn't exactly sound like a future record-breaker. But it wouldn't have been very useful to air the teenager's strengths and weaknesses publicly in any detail. Although they were extensive.

Freyss raves about how good Federer's forehand was even at 14: "His preparation for the shot was excellent: how perfectly he was positioned, how he brought down the top of the racket just before hitting the ball and then sped up the ball with his wrist. That wrist! He can do so much with it, give the ball more speed or spin at the very last second or change its direction." In his forehand, his priority as coach was to preserve it, do nothing which might impede the flow of that motion. His only direction to Federer was to swing through for longer for greater control.

His forehand is unmistakeable to this day, technically perfect and nonetheless unique, says Freyss. It's the jewel in Federer's crown. The American writer David Foster Wallace gushingly described it as a "great liquid whip". John Yandell, American tennis analyst and publisher of the online tennis magazine "tennisplayer.net", studied Federer's forehand over hours of video and distinguished 26 different variations of the stroke – when it comes to weight distribution, grip, the use of his wrist or his swing. This wealth of variation allows Federer to hit winners from anywhere. In terms of grip and swing, his forehand is fairly conservative and is thus recommendable for hobby players, too – it's the execution which makes it extraordinary.

But when it came to the 14-year-old's other strokes, Freyss had his work cut out for him. The topspin backhand was a particular weak point: "I had the feeling he was afraid to play it. He didn't have control of the ball, probably hadn't worked on it enough, because he tried to avoid it." There was a lot which was wrong with it: the preparation, the weight distribution, the placement of his legs and shoulders. In short: "We had to start the shot from scratch." Freyss noticed in particular that during the backhand slice, Federer pulled his head back on contact with the ball – as if showing his aversion to it unconsciously. Did Freyss ever consider changing Federer's backhand from a one- to a two-handed stroke? "No, that never came up. There were some things which were good, Roger had a good feel for the ball on his backhand side. If he'd added his left hand it would have thrown his whole game."

Federer himself had briefly considered changing to a two-handed backhand because he struggled to bring enough power to the ball and so mostly sliced it. At 12, he tried holding the racket with both hands at a juniors' tournament in France. "But it didn't really work. It hurt everywhere, in my chest, my wrist. I feel freer with a one-handed backhand. I'm happy with it," he says, looking back. From time to time he plays a few balls with a two-handed backhand during practice, just for fun – there are videos. It doesn't look so bad, but feels a little odd. As if someone else were playing with a Federer mask.

The public debate over whether he should be playing his backhand with one hand or two arose after it was far too late to change. Rafael Nadal knew more than anyone else how to exploit the one-handed Federer backhand – and two hands would have stabilised his weaker side. The American coaching legend Nick Bollettieri, mentor to stars like Andre Agassi, Jim Courier, Monica Seles or Maria Sharapova, speculated that Federer would have been even more successful with a two-handed backhand: "He might have been a player from Mars. Almost unbeatable." Heinz Günthardt, who has commentated countless numbers of the maestro's matches for Swiss television, vehemently disagrees: "Federer's running style is so aligned with his one-handed backhand. He often takes one last, long step to his backhand corner, which lets him reach balls a two-hander wouldn't be able to get to." In addition, a one-handed backhand is an advantage for his volley (because there's no need to change grip) and backhand slice. Günthardt concludes: "A one-handed backhand has certain advantages and disadvantages. But it fits brilliantly with Federer's game." And thanks to Nadal, who was always putting it to the test, Federer's topspin backhand is the stroke which has developed the most over his career.

Federer was a good, but also a difficult pupil, Freyss says looking back on their time in Ecublens: "Good because he immediately wanted to apply everything you'd talked about. He was unbelievably keen and eager to learn. Difficult because he quickly got angry if he didn't manage something." When it comes to his shots, Federer had learned so quickly that after a good year Freyss saw no reason why he couldn't make it to the very top. "But he was hot-tempered, quick to anger, easily frustrated. I worried it could get tough for him if he continued like that. But if he could solve that problem, I saw no more limits for him." The shots were all there, and he had never lacked creativity or a feel for the ball.

But as Federer began to get his temper under control (see Chapter 4), another problem presented itself: he had so many ways of winning points that he sometimes got confused – he was spoilt for choice of shot. And the ball travels so quickly that even a fraction of a second's hesitation can lose you the point. After his 2004 Wimbledon title, Federer reflected on this problem in an interview with The Observer: "My range of shots was a problem. You get a slow ball, and you think, 'What am I going to do with this?' If your game is limited, it's simple, you have a shot for each situation and you play it. I had too many options and I had to learn to choose the right shot and the right tactics, not just the most spectacular. I have to admit that when I joined the professional tour, I liked to think I was bringing something special and I would show off…" Lleyton Hewitt, his rival in his junior days, who had fewer options, already won the US Open at 20 and became number one in 2001. Federer was still finding himself at the time.

To this day, most tennis fans think that Federer plays primarily by instinct. But Craig O'Shannessy, the strategy analyst ("Brain Game Tennis") whose tactical advice helped Novak Djoković win titles in Wimbledon and the US Open in 2018 as well as the Australian Open 2019, disagrees vehemently: "Roger is constantly figuring out on a scale of risk: Do I really need this point or do I not? Do I go to a pattern that I want or do I go to a pattern that's a surprise? When he's up 30 love, a lot of times he will go to a strength of the opponent. But the opponent doesn't expect that. So even if he loses the point, Roger gets ahead in the mind game."

O'Shannessy even says: "A lot of my learning as a strategy analyst came from watching him." The Australian analyses the points at different scores, for example. He differentiates between primary and secondary patterns: the primary patterns are the central elements which make a player, the strengths he or she can rely on. For Federer, for instance, the outward serve followed by a forehand shot. Or to attack the opponent's backhand with his forehand. Patterns which have proven their worth year after year. For O'Shannessy, secondary patterns are those which a player chooses to bring in variation and surprise the opponent. Doing the same thing all the time makes you predictable.

92 So it's advisable to mix up the patterns. The strategy analyst takes Federer's serve as an example: "Roger loves to go wide on both sides with his serve. It brings the ball back on his forehand. But at 30 love he often goes down the middle. In the next service game, at love all, the opponent is thinking: Well, he did serve through the middle in the last service game. So what is he doing now? Roger completely confuses his opponent by being very strategic."

Either way, O'Shannessy argues, Federer's serve is one of the most underrated parts of his game. Probably because he doesn't have the sheer force of the most famous servers. But the analyst is convinced: "He's one of the greatest servers in the history of our sport. You can't read his serve. And he hits it so well. He's found the exact range of how hard he needs to hit it without redlining his power that he starts missing too much. And he brings a lot more factors into play with his serve. Especially, understanding where the opponent thinks it's going. Especially, looking for a serve plus one forehand. Especially, mixing in serve and volley." After all, Federer is also amongst the most successful when it comes to the number of aces. During Wimbledon

2017, he joined the 10,000 club – in third place after Goran Ivaniševič and 6 ft 11 in giant Ivo Karlović. "The service motion always came quite naturally to me," Federer says. "You could wake me up at three in the morning and I'd serve just as well as after warming up." The smoothness of his motion also meant he never had shoulder problems.

When Federer established himself on the professional circuit, he looked to his idols Pete Sampras, Stefan Edberg and Boris Becker, who had often sought a path to the net. When he beat Sampras in the fourth round at Wimbledon in 2001, he mostly played serve-and-volley, sticking close to the net. In his golden days, he then mostly relied on his superior game from the baseline. But when he lost his supremacy at the back of the court, he rediscovered his attacking tennis. His wide repertoire allows him to adjust his game. Whilst Hewitt is long-retired, Federer is still winning Grand Slam titles. In the autumn of his career, he might even be stronger than in his most successful times. That's certainly what his former coach Paul Annacone thinks. And Federer also shows that even in modern tennis, you can enjoy success with serve-and-volley and net play. "His volley was always good," says Freyss. "Nowadays he uses it more because he's realised that he needs to shorten the rallies."

For Günthardt, he's "daily proof that you can also play a little differently. He's actually quite an old-fashioned player. He shows that it's less about the style you cultivate but how well you understand the game you actually use. You can still be successful with slice today. But the ball has to be deployed correctly, in the right place, and slip

»Chairman Tim Phillips didn't have to think long about who to seat next to Queen Elizabeth II at lunch: Federer, of course.«

through. And you can also still win with serve-and-volley. That's what makes tennis so fascinating: it's full of secrets, it can't be mapped out."

O'Shannessy sees Federer as a timeless all-rounder who would have shone in the age of the wooden racket, too. For the tennis analyst, he's the ideal model: "I don't think enough players really study him enough. What makes this guy tick? Why is he winning matches? Why is he staying relevant? He's not a one-off. Study him! Copy him! I copy his patterns all the time. Roger's a huge one to copy. Because he has such an all-court game. He's not leaving any part of the court out. He's a great role model for our sport. But also on how to play the sport. How to be successful in this sport. And he's evolved with it. No question." Ivan Lendl once said Federer was the only one he watched for his shots – even in practice.

10. Float like a butterfly – Federer, the athlete

It's high time to tackle one of the greatest misconceptions about Roger Federer: that he was born with so much natural talent that his success came easily. That belief is all too understandable because he makes it all look so very easy. And the fallacy is reinforced by watching his relaxed practices during tournaments whilst Nadal races across the court on off-days, too, as if to catch up on everything he had neglected so far. But Federer's enormous amount of work takes place behind closed doors, during his training blocks. Günter Bresnik, who coached the rising Austrian star Dominic Thiem, tells a story: "I definitely know how hard Federer works. I knew him as a teenager. And I was there when he was preparing for the 2009 French Open with Stefan Koubek. Koubek was known as one of the fittest players on the tour. But after two days he said to me: 'Günter, I can't take it anymore. Either I do Federer's tennis training or his fitness training with him. I can't do both.'"

Rafael Nadal was also subject to the widespread belief that it all falls into Federer's lap. In his autobiography, "Rafa", he wrote: "I play through pain much of the time, but I think all elite sports people do. All except Federer, at any rate. I've had to push and mould my body to adapt it to cope with the repetitive muscular stress that tennis forces on you, but he seems to have been born to play the game. His physique – his DNA – seems perfectly adapted to tennis, rendering him immune to the injuries the rest of us are doomed to put up with. They tell me he doesn't train as hard as I do. I don't know if it's true, but it would figure."

98   Maybe Nadal needs to think that to boost his motivation against Federer. Maybe his opponent's brilliance as a player makes it easy to underestimate the work that he, too, has to put in. His fitness coach Pierre Paganini vehemently denies the idea that his protégé has it easier. In an interview with The New York Times after the 2012 season after which Federer's seventh Wimbledon victory made him the number one again for a few months, he explained that just because the physical side is less obvious than with others, like muscular Rafael Nadal or quick-footed Novak Djoković, doesn't mean it's less important. On the contrary. Paganini even believes that Federer has to work on his fitness level even more because he plays a more varied game. "Roger varies play a great deal. So if you vary a lot it means you also have to have footwork that is more varied. That means you have to train to adapt to his type of game." Paganini uses an analogy to show what he means: "Take someone who speaks English and French well and take someone else who speaks English, Russian, Japanese, Spanish and Chinese. Roger, for me, is the second one. He speaks lots of languages on the court with his creativity, but he also speaks lots of languages with his speed and co-ordination and his physique because he is obliged to do it because he is a creative player. What is more difficult? To speak seven languages or two? Seven, which proves that when you have lots of talent you have to work a lot, and that's what Roger does. He wouldn't be able to continue if he didn't like it."

Paganini was a stroke of luck for Federer, so much more than his fitness coach, also a friend and fatherly advisor. **99** Nothing important is decided without him. He met the talented young hotshot for the first time when he was 13. When Federer passed the admission test for Swiss Tennis' training programme in Ecublens in 1995, Paganini was the fitness trainer and administrative director. Federer proved himself over the three-day test with a twelve-minute run, fitness course, demonstration of his shots and a test match, coming in first place nationally. He was one of the four applicants who succeeded out of sixteen. But on a physical level, Paganini saw a lot of room for improvement. As administrative director, he also handled the choice of host family and in Federer's case, chose well with the Christinets. Without them, plagued by homesickness in the first few months and with only a smattering of French, the young boy from rural Basel would likely soon have abandoned his tennis training in French-speaking Switzerland.

Playing against the national competition, Federer easily compensated his athletic deficiencies with his talent. But although he was playful by nature and found little joy in monotonous drills, Paganini managed to get him excited about physical training by keeping the exercises as close to tennis as possible. He wasn't trying to build bulky biceps or produce 100-metre sprinters. The question at the back of Paganini's mind was: what use is it on the court? He developed a plan for Federer for the next three years, over the course of which he got him up to a respectable athletic level: at 17, Federer could keep up with regional sprinters for the first 30 metres, in his 12-minute runs he covered 3,300 metres, and he could squat 150 kg. So Paganini managed to bring together explosiveness, stamina and strength in his most talented student. Pleased with his progress, Federer hired the French-Swiss Paganini, who also speaks perfect Swiss German, as his personal fitness coach. Each season, Paganini worked with him for around 140 days of the year, later also 70 with Stan Wawrinka, who, since 2005, also puts his faith in him.

It's only because Federer prioritises his physical training that he is able to stay on top when in tennis terms, he's past retirement age. Every year he goes through three or four blocks – ideally one in February after the Australian Open, one before the clay court season, one after the US Open in September or October and one in the off-season in December. Add to that three to five individual training weeks throughout the year. The strenuous days of injury prevention exercises, warm-up, fitness training, tennis training and massage can easily run from 7.30 a.m. to 6 or 7 p.m. Since Federer doesn't share pictures of each training session on Twitter, Instagram or Snapchat, it's easy to get the impression that in between tournaments he's mostly relaxing on the beach or hiking in the alps with his family. Which, of course, isn't true.

An interesting detail is that Federer and Nadal, the most successful tennis players in history, are both officially 6 ft 1 in tall and weigh 187 lbs. And yet they are built completely differently. Where the Spaniard has a bodybuilder's arms, Federer's upper body is surprisingly lean, and he has strong, but not particularly bulky legs. Paginini rarely works with large weights, big muscles would only be a hindrance. "Federer's strength and weight are in perfect relation to one another," says Heinz Günthardt. "There are quicker players than him. But he anticipates well, he's agile and has excellent balance. That allows him to control the ball well, even if he only just reaches it and has to stretch out completely."

To really grasp Federer's excellent legwork, just try the following at his next match: for once, fix your eyes not on the ball but on his feet. Then you see how light-footed he is, how quickly he can change direction, how he positions himself perfectly to the ball with tiny steps. Tennis analyst Craig O'Shannessy says: "You forget how well he floats around the court. How well he uses the energy of the impact of his foot into the court and the energy out of the court. The flexing of the ankles, the flexing of the knees, the movement of the hips. He is a master at providing minimal wear and tear on his body by floating around the court and interacting with the court in a way that just doesn't hurt him. It's amazing to see. I have no idea how to teach it. He is the absolute master of playing tennis at the highest level while being the ultimate minimalist with the energy he expends around the court and the energy he expends to make the shot. That's the key to his longevity by far." You can't help but think of boxer Muhammad Ali's famous line "float like a butterfly, sting like a bee". Federer floats across the court and then, usually with his forehand, he stings.

John McEnroe, once feared for his angry outbursts on court, now renowned for his trenchant TV commentary, admiringly describes Federer as the Baryshnikov of tennis. The Soviet ballet dancer Mikhail Baryshnikov was considered one of the most graceful of his peers and, having moved to North America, found fame as a choreographer and guest on the television series "Sex and the City". The likening of Federer to a ballet dancer, a comparison Paganini also likes to make, is fitting, as it's his lightness and balance which are striking. Or actually aren't, because they seem so natural. Federer's legwork is only really noticeable when it's off somehow. When he's a fraction of a second late to the ball, or off-balance. Then, all of a sudden, he seems profane, like a wizard without his wand. He himself says: "It's my fitness which allows me to play as I do today. Without the physical work that wouldn't have been possible. All of a sudden, I reached balls I wouldn't have before. And my talent, my hand-eye coordination and my technique then allowed me shots which I never thought I would have been able to play. That's when it started to get really fun. Then I was running at full speed."

The groundwork for his fitness is laid during his longer training blocks with Paganini. It's therefore no coincidence that he had his first major crisis in 2008 because the mononucleosis which had struck the December before prevented him from training properly. And when, after the 83 matches of the successful but intensive season of 2012, he added a 10-day South American tour with exhibition matches in São Paulo, Buenos Aires and Bogotá, he paid the price. The following year, his back flared up again, and he lost his usual spark. That goes to show that like everyone else, he can't take the balance in his body for granted.

When Nadal wrote in his autobiography that his rival was immune to injury, that, of course, also wasn't true. It's also thanks to his consistent training and planning that he is almost never seriously injured and usually has his weak point, his back, under control. His degree of care towards his body is evident in the fact that over 1,400 professional matches, he has never had to retire. Time and time again he takes the necessary time to build up and recover and consistently takes injury prevention measures. Smart planning also means sacrifices. After Wimbledon 2016, he took a five-month break because his knee hadn't quite recovered from the meniscus surgery and the injury had a knock-on effect, straining other areas. It pained him to miss the Olympic Games in Rio. But in early 2017, he quickly got back to full speed.

In Federer, Paganini had found an eager but demanding student who thought for himself and didn't just reel off what was demanded. In an interview with the New York Times, the fitness coach said: "In 2000, when we started working full-time again, I proposed a complex thing and sensed while he was doing it that it was more and more perfect. He then explained at the end why I had asked him to do it. It was fascinating to me. He had understood as an athlete how to do it but also understood why. He had the internal and external aspects covered. He's not someone who consumes. He's someone who creates." It wasn't unusual for Federer to suggest variations on exercises to stress other things. Whilst as a young man he had been an artist who wanted nothing more than to play tennis, he became one who knew precisely what he needed to express his virtuosity, says Paganini.

Paganini offered a peek at the work behind the scenes during an interview with the Zurich-based Tages-Anzeiger in November 2016, when they were working on Federer's comeback. "What I found fascinating all over again was how delighted Roger is at even the smallest bit of progress. When someone like him, who loves to play tennis so much and hasn't been able to play tournaments for months, comes to practice with a smile on his face, it's more than passion. He really is one of a kind. He owes nothing to anyone and yet he works every day as if he owed it to the world. So seriously, so intensely and yet in such an easy-going way."

Paganini only rarely travels to tournaments with Federer, his work happens beforehand. On tour, he's taken care of by physiotherapist Daniel Troxler. Federer met him early on, at the Sydney Olympic Games in 2000, when Troxler worked for Swiss Olympic. The former track-and-field athlete had worked with Swiss marathon runner Viktor Röthlin, and after Röthlin's retirement, Federer brought him on board in 2014. "He has magic hands," raves the tennis pro.

Federer grew up playing a host of sports. Next to tennis he also played football (soccer), handball, basketball and table tennis. He liked football in particular, playing for FC Concordia Basel – naturally as a striker. At 12, he had had to choose between the sports because the training volume was too much. He opted for tennis, having already enjoyed national success early on. Paganini is convinced that his coordination skills would also have made for a good football player. With his versatility, the fitness coach believes he could also have been a sprinter, volleyball player or skier. Or even a javelin thrower. Good thing he chose tennis.

11. Mozart and Metallica – the phenomenon

Great literature is timeless. And such is the nature of American writer David Foster Wallace's 6,000-word essay "Roger Federer as Religious Experience", written in the summer of 2006. Much has happened in the tennis world since then, but the essay remains unparalleled and has lost none of its salience. Foster Wallace, who had himself played well as a junior and had already written several excellent pieces on his favourite sport, was sent to Wimbledon by the New York Times, charged with writing a longer piece on Federer. It was printed in late August, before the US Open, in Play Magazine, a sports supplement.

Foster Wallace was a rising literary star whose 1,000-page epic "Infinite Jest", a novel dealing with addiction in all its forms, is considered a milestone in American literature. Tennis already played a central role in the 1996 novel, which is set at the fictional Enfield Tennis Academy in Boston. Amongst other things, Foster Wallace has a tennis coach ponder that "the true opponent, the enfolding boundary, is the player himself. Always and only the self out there, on court, to be met, fought, brought to the table to hammer out terms. The competing boy on the net's other side: he is not the foe: he is more the partner in the dance. He is the what is the word excuse or occasion for meeting the self. As you are his occasion. Tennis's beauty's infinite roots are self-competitive. You compete with your own limits to transcend the self in imagination and execution." And further: "You seek to vanquish and transcend the limited self whose limits make the game possible in the first place. It is tragic and sad and chaotic and lovely. All life is the same, as citizens of the human State: the animating limits are within, to be killed and mourned, over and over again." Tennis as an allegory for life – an interesting thought.

It was therefore a safe assumption that if Foster Wallace dared to take on Federer, even going to see him in the Garden of Eden of tennis, something exceptional would emerge. And he didn't disappoint. Foster Wallace coined the term "Federer Moment": "These are times, as you watch the young Swiss play, when the jaw drops and eyes protrude and sounds are made that bring spouses in from other rooms to see if you're O.K. The Moments are more intense if you've played enough tennis to understand the impossibility of what you just saw him do." Foster Wallace goes on to describe a rally from the 2005 US Open final against Andre Agassi: Federer dances backwards like a ballerina to hit a winning forehand down the line, out of his backhand corner. It's a rally of 11 seconds which to most could look like any other, but the writer was enthralled by his sporting hero's control over his own body. Foster Wallace had seen that match, like many others, on television. When he first saw him play live, it left a deep impression. Because, as he wrote: "The truth is that TV tennis is to live tennis pretty much as video porn is to the felt reality of human love. (...) If you've watched tennis only on television, you simply have no idea how hard these pros are hitting the ball, how fast the ball is moving, how little time the players have to get to it, and how quickly they're able to move and rotate and strike and recover. And none are faster, or more deceptively effortless about it, than Roger Federer." What

comes across more on television than in the stadium, however, is his intelligence – because that often reveals itself in angles: "Federer is able to see, or create, gaps and angles for winners that no one else can envision, and television's perspective is perfect for viewing and reviewing these Federer Moments."

The driver of the press bus which took Foster Wallace to the All England Club in 2006 promised him that seeing Federer live was a "bloody near-religious experience" – thus unwittingly naming the most famous tennis essay of all time. There are two explanations, writes Foster Wallace, for Federer's supremacy: a technical one (preferred by journalists) and a mysterious, metaphysical one. As a writer, he chose the latter: "The metaphysical explanation is that Roger Federer is one of those rare, preternatural athletes who appear to be exempt, at least in part, from certain physical laws. Good analogues here include Michael Jordan, who could not only jump inhumanly high but actually hang there a beat or two longer than gravity allows, and Muhammad Ali, who really could 'float' across the canvas and land two or three jabs in the clock-time required for one. There are probably a half-dozen other examples since 1960. And Federer is of this type – a type that one could call genius, or mutant, or avatar. He is never hurried or off-balance. The approaching ball hangs, for him, a split-second longer than it ought to. His movements are lithe rather than athletic. Like Ali, Jordan, Maradona, and Gretzky, he seems both less and more substantial than the men he faces. Particularly in the all-white that Wimbledon enjoys getting away with still requiring, he looks like what **109** he may well (I think) be: a creature whose body is both flesh and, somehow, light." If this conjures the image of Jesus in your mind's eye, that's probably intentional. Federer as religious experience.

Foster Wallace also met Federer personally at the All England Club for a 20-minute one-on-one interview. He was less interested in his answers than in getting a feel for the person. He noticed that Federer peppered his sentences with "you knows" and "maybes", which reminded him how terribly young the player still was. And, on shaking it, Federer's hand felt "like a carpentry rasp". His overall impression, recorded in a footnote, is "that Roger Federer is either a very nice guy or a guy who's very good at dealing with the media – or (most likely) both." What captivated Foster Wallace, however, is not the person, but the tennis player. Federer was proof of his theory that beauty may not be the goal of professional sports, but can often be found there. And Foster Wallace was grateful that, in the era of power-baseline tennis, Federer has turned back time, bringing back a touch and finesse not seen since John McEnroe.

The depth of the author's detail shows how intensively he has studied tennis. He retraces how the greater importance of the ground strokes through graphite rackets and heavier topspin, together with greater athleticism, have combined to make tennis monotonous. He describes the seemingly awkward but mercilessly powerful and athletic Ivan Lendl as the progenitor of this style; an athlete as easily replicable as the racket itself. But thanks to Federer, Foster Wallace writes, we now know that this is not the end of line: "Roger Federer is now dominating the largest, strongest, fittest, best-trained and -coached field of male pros who've ever existed, with everyone using a kind of nuclear racket that's said to have made the finer calibrations of kinaesthetic sense irrelevant, like trying to whistle Mozart during a Metallica concert." So Federer is both Metallica and Mozart – surely an impossible combination. Or, to quote Foster Wallace again: "Roger Federer is a first-rate, kick-ass power-baseliner. It's just that that's not all he is. There's also his intelligence, his occult anticipation, his court sense, his ability to read and manipulate opponents, to mix spins and speeds, to misdirect and disguise, to use tactical foresight and peripheral vision and kinaesthetic range instead of just rote pace." And he does it all with the consistency and relentlessness of an Ivan Lendl.

The imaginative tennis lover had little love for Nadal. Like probably many Federer fans, he saw him primarily as a threat: "For reasons that are not well understood, war's codes are safer for most of us than love's. You too may find them so, in which case Spain's mesomorphic and totally martial Rafael Nadal is the man's man for you – he of the unsleeved biceps and Kabuki self-exhortations." Foster Wallace was delighted that Federer claimed victory against Nadal in the 2006 Wimbledon final. He closes his Federer essay with the words: "Genius is not replicable. Inspiration, though, is contagious, and multiform – and even just to see, close up, power and aggression made vulnerable to beauty is to feel inspired and (in a fleeting, mortal way) reconciled."

But in the following years, the writer was forced to acknowledge how the balance of power shifted towards Nadal – until, in 2008, Nadal toppled the king from his throne. Foster Wallace battled depression for 30 years, and for a long time he was able to manage it through medication. On the 12th of September 2008, he took his own life, aged 46. Four days earlier, Federer had won the US Open for the fifth time in a row.

Much has been written about Federer: more than 50 books. There are biographical, poetic, philosophical, self-centred, humorous, obsessive, illustrated, technical and even erotic pieces on the athlete. But what is it which makes that Foster Wallace essay so extraordinary that more than 12 years later, it is still rightly considered the ultimate one? It's that the American's fascination with tennis and its players can be felt in every line. His experience as a talented junior player let him cut through the subject intellectually, whilst his writing and imagination let him draw observations from tennis which go well beyond it. Foster Wallace captured what it is which makes Federer so fascinating, and every line still holds true today. Writers who know nothing of tennis try to elevate the sports virtuoso to a higher plane, transferring ideas or concepts of great writers (like Shakespeare) or philosophers (like Kant) onto him: pure coquetry.

Foster Wallace didn't. He always began from tennis itself, from his precise observations and experiences – and drew conclusions which cast Federer in an altogether different light. Foster Wallace was himself a good junior player, but not good enough to hope for a career in professional tennis. At 14, he was number 17 in the Midwest; by 18, he had dropped off every interregional ranking. But the sport's grip on him never loosened. Tennis is a major theme not just in his excellent read, "Infinite Jest"; his other essays on tennis were compiled in the volume "String Theory" and are warmly recommended to all.

Were you to pen a novel about a tennis whizz, you would hardly choose a biography like Federer's, smooth and almost without crises. You'd more likely create a protagonist in the style of Boris Becker, one of striking strengths and weaknesses. But Federer's appeal lies elsewhere – the beauty of his game, his boundless passion and surprising groundedness. Even the South African Nobel Laureate in Literature, John Maxwell Coetzee, revealed himself as an enormous Federer fan in his public exchange of letters with his American colleague Paul Auster ("Here and Now: Letters, 2008–2011"). He could, he writes, scrutinise Federer's golden days again and again, "revisiting them in memory". And then he wonders what it is which triggers such intensity of feeling: "I have just seen something that is at the same time both human and more than human; I have just seen something like the human ideal made visible." Moreover: "One starts by envying Federer, one moves from there to admiring him and one ends up neither envying him or admiring him but exalted at the revelation of what a human being – a being like oneself – can do." Watching Federer, wrote Coetzee, felt like studying a masterwork of art.

But it must be added that artful play is worthless if it can't compete in the merciless contest of styles, characters and athletes. Coetzee's fellow writer Paul Auster agrees on the subject of Federer, also explicitly referring to his glory days: "As for the exaltation you talk about when watching Federer in his glory days, I am in total accord with you. Awe at the fact that a fellow human being is accomplishing such things, that we (as a species) are not only the worms we often appear to be but are also capable of achieving miraculous things – in tennis, in music, in poetry, in science – and that envy and admiration dissolve into a feeling of overwhelming joy."

His white bandana wrapped around his head, Foster Wallace would have gently nodded.

12. It must be love

When the tennis elite was dashing across the courts in Flushing Meadows in Queens, New York, in early September 2016, Roger Federer went hiking in the mountains around Appenzell. He shared photos of himself against a picturesque backdrop on social media. Him posing in front of an idyllic lake, venturing into a dripstone cave, climbing up to the famous Aescher Mountain Inn, enjoying the view and taking a break on a bench in front of a wooden hut, his rucksack set down at his side. Pictures which could have been from a campaign for Switzerland Tourism. Having decided to cancel the season after Wimbledon because of his injured knee, Federer spent other days swimming with his children or playing a round of crazy golf. The sight of Federer wandering along with a relaxed expression and stubble on his face almost made you worry that he was enjoying it too much to return to the professional tour. Gone would be the stress of constant travel, the pressure of performing in front of millions of television viewers, the exhausting practice sessions.

"Tennis years are dog years," Boris Becker once said. And at over 1,300 professional matches, Federer had already played significantly more than the German had in his entire career (927). Federer has long achieved financial security, his countless records leave nothing to prove, he has a wife and four children who like spending time with him, and his own foundation and involvement in the management agency Team 8 could keep him perfectly busy. We should also be realistic: at the time, Federer's last Grand Slam title – Wimbledon 2012 – was already four years ago, and he wasn't getting any younger. The signs from his body were clear. But despite it all, at 35, he wouldn't have dreamed of stopping. Which only leaves one conclusion: it must be love. His love of tennis.

It's easy to love the sport when you're mopping the floor with the competition. But what about when you start losing more and more often? When you reach your limits, suffer, despair? When the voices saying it would be better to put down the racket get louder? In his worst season since reaching the global elite, Federer reflected on his relationship with tennis at the 2013 US Open. Asked how motivated he still was, he responded: "Clearly when you win everything, it's fun. That doesn't necessarily mean you love the game more. You just like winning, being on the front page, lifting trophies, doing comfortable press conferences. It's nice. But that doesn't mean you really actually love it, love it. That maybe shines through more in times when you don't play that well. For me, I knew it, winning or losing, practice court or match court, that I love it." The fact that didn't change when he wasn't winning so often is an homage to the sport in its purest form.

It's in practice that you can really see how smitten he is with the little yellow balls, even after all these years. In those moments, much more than during his matches, you can see how playful he is, how he gently strokes them, sometimes serving ever so gently, sometimes playing high, sometimes flat, with feeling, then force, trying crazy shots, looking for special angles. And that's how, in a sport played since the 19th century, he even discovered a new shot. It was mid-August 2015 and he was finishing off his first training session in Cincinnati before one of his favourite tournaments. He was still jet-lagged, his training partner Benoît Paire suffering from an ear infection. They were about to finish, just playing a few more points to finish the training block.

On a whim, Federer jumped forward to the service line whilst returning and hit the ball immediately after it bounced. An almost impossible feat: the ball was rushing towards him at a horrendous speed and it took excellent hand-eye coordination to control it. His trick quickly earned him a few points. A new stroke was born, and he christened it after himself: "Sneak Attack By Roger", or SABR for short, because Federer sneaks forward to attack the ball when returning. The shot didn't revolutionise tennis, and Federer quickly stopped using it regularly. But the fact that he even invented it and integrated it as a surprising variation in his matches shows how playful and curious he still is after all these years.

For Mats Wilander, the seven-time Grand Slam champion who had had enough of tennis at 32, this is the most fascinating thing about Federer. In a piece in the New York Times before the 2017 US Open on Federer's miraculous resurrection, he was quoted as follows: "I always tell people that when you watch Federer, don't just watch him play the point. Watch what he does in between points. He's always fiddling with a tennis ball or with his racket, and he's hitting an extra shot, trying some crazy drop shot when the point is over, or flicking the ball to a ball kid after a missed serve. Nobody else does that. Nobody has ever done that. And he still does it. Wimbledon final – it doesn't matter. He just seems to enjoy the feeling of having the ball on his strings."

Christophe Freyss, the former Swiss national coach, makes a similar observation: "When Roger plays the ball to the ball boys, it always lands right in their hands. Even when they're in the far corner of the court," the Frenchman tells the Swiss newspaper Le Matin. He goes on: "That childlike joy will be with him all his life. It's his greatest piece of good fortune. Many others lost that joy over the years. He didn't." His coach Severin Lüthi says that on the court, Federer still seems like an 18-year-old, even though he's twice that age. "He just loves to play. He's like a little boy. There are plenty of others who are in peak physical form, talented, mentally strong. But they don't have that unwavering passion. It's an enormous source of energy."

Federer's fellow players, past and present, say again and again how astonishing it is that despite all his success, he hasn't had enough. "Others would long have been content with a couple of Grand Slam titles and having made good money," says Mark Philippoussis, his opponent in his first

» It's in practice that you can really see how smitten he is with the little yellow balls, even after all these years. **«**

Wimbledon final. "But he is still hungry after so many major wins. He still wants to win more and break more records. My only explanation is his deep love for this sport." John McEnroe raves: "I've never seen someone love playing as much as Roger. That's the thing what I admire more than anything about him. The one thing I wish I could have taken from him is his joie de vivre. He's so competitive but is able to shrug off his losses so well." In his second auto-biography ("But Seriously"), which deals with his life after retirement, the American writes how it touches him to see Federer moved to tears by tennis. "God knows, Roger has cried more than any other top player, but they are genuine tears. No faking emotions there, it really means that much to him. I never cried when I won. I cried on other occasions on court – under a towel, no one ever saw me – when my first marriage was breaking up, when the outside stresses of life were taking over my mind and affecting my tennis so much I could hardly play, but I never cried from relief at winning. I guess that's one more reason why Roger is so special: after all these years, he's still insatiably hungry for more titles."

For Heinz Günthardt, who has known him for over 20 years, Federer has found the perfect mix: "What has always impressed me is his incredible ambition, which of course you need for that level of discipline. And at the same time the ease he shows. How he handles pressure. When you look at Rafael Nadal: he's constantly battling himself. So is Novak Djoković. They need so much more energy to perform. And I don't so much mean the energy on the court, but the energy off-court. They find it much harder to switch off than he does. With him you feel he's doing exactly what he loves. You never hear him complain that it's too much." Is that an attitude you can teach young players? Günthardt shrugs. "I don't know how. I think that's just his personality. You can achieve a lot through training. But he's just born to play tennis."

But the moments under the floodlights are just the tip of the iceberg. It takes countless hours of preparation and many a sacrifice to get there. After every match, you have to face critical questions – whether you want to or not. When you miss an easy forehand, it can follow you for weeks, even months. And only few athletes go around the world as often as the tennis pros. It's a draining life, physically and mentally. Pete Sampras, one of Federer's former idols, was burned out by 31 and retired. Paul Annacone took Sampras to his last triumph at the 2002 US Open and was later Federer's coach from 2010 to 2013. Nowhere were the two more different than in their response to all the public attention. The bustle around Federer at any given moment is unimaginable. When he's out in public, he doesn't have a single moment of peace: "Travelling with him is like travelling with a superhero or a rock star. But he's found a way to make a very abnormal environment feel normal to him. He's done that like a true magician. And he's so good at not wasting energy at things he cannot control. It just doesn't bother him."

The fact that his love of tennis hasn't cooled is also thanks to his careful planning. When he's off tour, he switches off completely. He can put down the racket for days at a time and just lie on the beach. Despite his appetite for tennis, he manages to maintain his work-life balance. But before his five-month tournament break in July 2016, there were signs he was losing his enjoyment. Less on the court than in the side effects of that life. At press conferences it was clear that he no longer felt like answering the same questions over and over again. From time to time he seemed grumpy – highly unusual for him. Taking a longer break from the global tennis circus for a few months to regain his energy and motivation was good not just for his damaged knee, but also for his head.

When, in January 2017, he returned to the tour, his body and spirit seemed as refreshed as after a long spa holiday. He won his 18th Grand Slam title in Melbourne, the 19th and 20th followed soon after. The break was like a dip in the Fountain of Youth. And, in 2019, his journey through the Centre Courts of the world continues. He has plenty of time for hiking later.

13. 869 hours to the triple-digit club

Among the many who congratulated Roger Federer after claiming his 100th title in Dubai in early March 2019 was his former peer James Blake. He tweeted playfully: "Just watched @rogerfederer win his 100th title and my daughter asked 'how many did you win?' '10' I responded proudly. 'How come you only won 10? That's like none.' Thanks, Roger, for making me look bad in front of my kids. Congrats."

What would Federer have said on the 13th of February 2000 in Marseille if you had told him that he would one day reach 100 titles, and go beyond even that? On that day, he wept bitterly after losing his first ATP final against his compatriot, good friend and PlayStation rival Marc Rosset in the tiebreak of the third set. Looking back, Rosset says he felt for Federer. And tried to comfort him. At the trophy ceremony he told him: "Don't worry, you'll go on to win tournaments." But the words rang hollow. Sure, that's easy for Rosset to say, the teenager thought to himself. And a dark thought crossed his mind: perhaps he would never have another opportunity like that again. But for the photographers, he finally managed to muster up a smile, dressed in an old grey jumper, mini-trophy in hand.

Federer had to wait another year before finally winning his first ATP tournament on the 4th of February 2001 in Milan – in his third final. It wasn't a match for the ages against Frenchman Julien Boutter, Federer had delivered his masterpiece in the semi-final against Olympic champion and top 10 player Yevgeny Kafelnikov, despite having been plagued by an aching wisdom tooth for days. The final against Boutter was tarnished a little by a mishap of the umpire, Lars Graff. After the tiebreak of the second set, he wrongly told the Frenchman to serve first, rather than Federer. Boutter obeyed but was so confused that he lost his serve right away – which eventually proved decisive. Federer's parents had driven the 210 miles from Basel to catch the premiere. His father Robert was so nervous that he locked the car key in the car, making the drive back to Basel cold and windy thanks to the window they'd had to break to reclaim it. But the parents' trip to the capital of Lombardy paid off. From the stands they watched their son, just 19 years and 180 days old, lift up a trophy at a professional tournament for the very first time. The weighty trophy bore a laurel wreath – a harbinger of the victories which had only just begun for the teenager.

Around 18 years – or exactly 6,601 days – later in Dubai, Federer looked back on his first tournament victory: "I was so relieved I was not going to be that guy who was going to be an endless talent with no titles. You can imagine today sitting with 100 how much disbelief there is in between what happened then and now." Federer collected his 100 titles over 19 countries, 30 cities and 548 matches, of which he won six by walkover and lost one: at the 2007 Masters Cup in Shanghai, where he lost his first group match against Chilean Fernando González but still went on to win the tournament. The BBC painstakingly assembled further numbers to capture his 100-title milestone: it took him 83,302 rallies, of which he won 46,508 – or 55.83%. That includes 4,378 aces. And he spent 52,152 minutes on court, a little over 869 hours or over 36 days. That's the time it would take to watch all six seasons and 86 episodes of gangster drama The Sopranos 10 times over. No offence to mafia boss Tony Soprano, but watching Federer chase his titles was more gripping, entertaining and a little less re-petitive. Even against a familiar backdrop, he never failed to surprise.

In the modern age of tennis, Grand Slam titles have become the ultimate benchmark. But for Federer, the triple-digit title number carries a particular satisfaction be-cause it shows that his commitment extends beyond the big stages. As he emphasises in Dubai, he spends most of his time, after all, on the ATP Tour and not at Grand Slam tour-naments. And what does he think was the key to winning all these titles? His explanation is elaborate: "You have to be fit on many fronts: mentally, physically, also your game has to translate. You have to be able to beat different types of play-ers, not just the grinders, not just the big servers, not just the attacking players. You have to be able to beat them all in successive days. I think that's a tricky thing to do for a lot of players. Only a few can do that every year, five, six, seven times or more during a single year. For that you need to be able to adapt your game to conditions, got to be able to play through the pain because I've been hurt or sick many times during events that I ended up winning. Some of them being slams, as well."

For years, Federer played with the regularity of Swiss clockwork. He participated in 65 consecutive Grand Slam tournaments, from the 2001 US Open to the 2016 Australian Open. From October 2003 (Vienna) to October 2005 (Bangkok) he won 24 finals in a row. In the years 2004, 2005 and 2006 alone he amassed 34 titles. And his 23 successive semi-finals at Grand Slam events from Wimbledon 2004 to the 2010 Australian Open may well be a record for the ages. Number two is Novak Djoković with 14, Rafael Nadal just managed 5 in a row. "In terms of my game, I think I needed to get really match tough to be able to be at 100% every single day," Federer adds to his recipe for success in Dubai. "That was not easy for me. Check my emotions, that was not easy. Eventually I figured that part out. Then not wasting too much energy throughout the tournament. I remember in the beginning of my career, by the time the quarters came around, I was quite exhausted already because I was so happy winning points, disappointed losing points, I would get to the quarters and be tired."

Severin Lüthi was Federer's coach for more than half of his titles and says: "100 is an unbelievable number. It's not something you can aim for. That's 10 titles a year for 10 years. Or 5 for 20 years. Unbelievable! The most important thing is that Roger loves the game so much. His passion has always driven him." In all those years, Lüthi says,

Federer had never bailed on practice because he didn't feel like it. "Of course, not every practice is equally good. Sometimes he doesn't feel like it, is less on top of things. But he always finds a way to have fun. You can play from the baseline for 20 minutes and he will do something different with each ball. He'll play one with extreme topspin, the next one with slice, sometimes he even groans differently with each stroke. Or he imitates other players. When you're in practice with him, you don't feel like you're on court with an older player. When I see young players who monotonously play the same ball in training, for them it's work, for Roger it's a game. And it helps that he kept his feet on the ground. He knows what a privileged life he leads. The world is his oyster, but he's very aware of his luck with tennis. There are others who have won much less than him who struggle with that."

There is, however, one player in the open era who has lifted the trophy even more often: Jimmy Connors with his 109 tournament wins. After Federer joined the 100 club, the American tweeted: "Welcome to the 'Triple Digit' tournament victory club @rogerfederer – I've been a bit lonely – glad to have the company!!!" At the same time, Connors makes no secret of wanting to keep the record. As different as they are, they share their passion for their sport. Connors played his final match on the professional tour at 43 and in 2001 played in the semi-finals of the US Open aged 39. His quarter-final against Aaron Krickstein, 15 years his junior, whom he wrestled down in the fifth set after being down 2-5, symbolised his determination, which never waned with age. The match became a CBS classic, used to bridge the rain breaks during the US Open. Now that the largest stadiums at Flushing Meadows have been equipped with retractable roofs, tennis fans have to revert to YouTube to relive the dramatic comeback.

Connors collected his titles between 1972 and 1989 in 15 different seasons and with a preference for indoor courts. Federer has reached 18 seasons with at least one title. It was only in 2016, the year of his knee operation, that he went home empty-handed. It's extremely tempting to compare the two trophy collections. But since Connors played in various tournament series which no longer exist, it's hard to make a serious comparison. What's clear is that Federer was more successful at Grand Slam tournaments (20-8) and has more higher-tier titles. The difficulty of comparing players from different eras, however, is apparent when you consider that Rod Laver "only" racked up 74 titles in the professional era, but had celebrated 126 as an amateur and a pro beforehand. With 200 tournament victories, "The Rocket" should be seen as the most successful player of all.

At any rate, Federer is hot on Connors' heels and celebrated his 101st title at the end of March 2019 in Miami. Much to the delight of James Blake, by the way, who congratulated him again. This time not on social media, but directly on court – as the tournament director of the Miami Open.

14. The Clooney of the sporting world – Federer, the brand

King Roger heads to work, his bag coolly slung over his right shoulder. He hardly notices the people around him, nodding absently, already focused. Just a few more steps to the glittering spotlights. He breathes deeply, and it begins with the words "Ciao Roger" and a white apron flying towards him. Today he's not playing tennis, he's making pasta with Italian chef Davide Oldani. Roger's brought along a few packets of Spaghetti No. 5 in his bag. "The secret is just to keep things simple," Oldani says with a thick Italian accent. His celebrity pupil nods obediently and proves nimble-fingered when chopping tomatoes, carrots and other vegetables. (A double was used for the high-speed chopping. The tennis pro still needs his fingers!) Their cheerful cooking is accompanied by Mikis Theodorakis' sirtaki music (atmospheric, but a little unfitting), and the crowning moment is Roger dropping a mint leaf which floats down to the tower of spaghetti – precise as a serve on the line on his opponent's break point.

Barilla reached deep into their pockets for the campaign, called "Masters of Pasta". In spring 2017, the global market leader made Federer their global brand ambassador. In the early nineties, Steffi Graf posed seductively in a black evening dress to boost German pasta sales, and now Federer is supposed to lend Barilla Pasta that special something. Forbes magazine speculates that the deal is worth around USD 40 million over five years. Federer's role as spaghetti seller shows how his manager, Tony Godsick, prepares his clients for advertising work after their retirement. And in July 2018, another major contract arrived just in time for Wimbledon: Federer has signed with Japanese clothing brand Uniqlo for 10 years. There are whispers of USD 300 million. Even if it were "just" half that, as the experts believe, it would still be an enormous amount for a tennis pro who won't be swinging a racket forever. But unlike for Federer's former outfitter, Nike, that's not all that important to Uniqlo. Federer won't just showcase their sportswear, but their leisurewear, too, using his fame to propel their expansion in the Western market.

A day in the life of Federer the advertising brand could look more or less as follows: After getting up, he makes himself a double espresso with his Jura coffee machine and eats a Lindt chocolate along with it. He looks at his Rolex and sees that he's running late. Using his Sunrise-operated phone, he calls his coach to tell him when they're meeting at the airport. He quickly packs his Wilson rackets and Uniqlo tennis gear in a bag and pays a few bills online with Credit Suisse before getting into his Mercedes estate car to drive to the airport with his family. A plane from NetJets, the US private business jet company, awaits him on the tarmac. Up in the clouds, he treats himself to a glass of Moët &

Chandon champagne and loads up on carbohydrates with a Barilla pasta lunch.

According to Forbes, this colourful mixture of advertising partners brought Federer the tidy sum of USD 65 million between June 2016 and Jun2017. That makes him the global number one among sportsmen in terms of sponsoring, beating basketball player LeBron James (USD 52 million) and footballer Cristiano Ronaldo (USD 47 million). In tennis, Kei Nishikori from Japan (USD 33 million), Rafael Nadal (USD 27 million) and Novak Djoković (USD 22 million) come closest. The Forbes estimates aren't an exact science, but Federer's lead is so large that there's no doubt he holds the top spot. When you add USD 12.2 million in prize money, he made USD 77.2 million in that year – his own record.

Since other sports offer higher prize money, appearance fees or salaries, he was "only" number seven of all athletes. The top earner was the boxer Floyd Mayweather (USD 285 million), ahead of footballers Lionel Messi(USD 111 million) and Ronaldo (USD 108 million). The fact that there were six sportsmen who earned more will hardly keep Federer up at night. In tennis terms, he opened a whole new dimension. Over his entire career, including appearance fees, he has probably made around USD 800 million, of which not even a sixth is prize money (USD 122 million, as per March 2019).

Apart from his sporting success, what is it that makes him so marketable? "For me, he's a phenomenon in this area, too," says marketing professor Torsten Tomczak, a branding specialist who lectures at the University of St.

Gallen. "My impression, which the whole planet seems to share: He is who he appears to be. Everyone likes to use the word authentic. I don't know if he really is like that in person. But he can at the very least maintain a public persona which is completely consistent. At every appearance. He never breaks character. And it's rare for someone to manage that." From a branding perspective, Federer is an "all-purpose tool", Tomczak explains: "the beautiful

thing about him: he fits almost everywhere, he's unbelievably versatile. He stands for quality and reliability, but exudes so much more. In the premium sector he operates at the same level as George Clooney, who stands for luxury. Not like a rapper who's living the high life, but rather class. For years, the question for luxury brands has been: Do we take Clooney or Federer? There aren't many at that level." At the same time, he says, Federer stands for classic family values: "He's married, has a tough job and still makes time to look after the kids. And he gets on well with his parents." That makes him a good fit for a brand like Barilla, who are in every family's kitchen cupboard.

It doesn't feel inconsistent for Federer to advertise the Swiss telecom company Sunrise (ad slogan: "Roger and I"), which tries to push that it's value for money, and at the same time luxury Rolex watches or Moët & Chandon, the market leader for champagne. His change from the hip Nike to Uniqlo, which sells affordable everyday clothing, was met with understanding among his fans. "Federer is the ideal partner to raise the Uniqlo brand's profile in the West," says Tomczak. As brand ambassadors, athletes compete with

Hollywood stars, he explains: "Sports move the world, and famous athletes embody the basic message of what everyone wants: success. Brands want to be associated with success. If Federer had won less, we wouldn't be talking about him. It's more complex with Hollywood stars. They represent beauty, a lifestyle."

Using brand ambassadors whose image rubs off on the product is not without risk, as the cases of Tiger Woods (an infidelity scandal) or Maria Sharapova (doping) show. But with Federer, who's seen as a control freak, the odds of him destroying his brand with careless words or deeds is minimal. Based on his observations, Tomczak concludes: "Federer is highly intelligent and willing to take advice. He might have overdone it at Wimbledon with his extravagant tennis kit in the past, but he's learned better."

The fact that his social media presence seems a bit homespun seems to fit quite well. It would feel strange if his manager, like Nadal's, wrote his tweets. If Federer feels like tweeting or posting a picture on Instagram, he does. If not, there can be radio silence on his channels for weeks. Though he used Facebook early on as a source of information for his fans, he joined Twitter and Instagram fairly late. At "only" 12.4 million followers, he's far behind Cristiano Ronaldo (77.2 million) on Twitter. And even further behind on Instagram (5.8 million compared to 159 million).

His social media behaviour is definitely in line with his personality, according to Tomczak. "But if you want to say something negative: Federer isn't one for the kids. Who follows Ronaldo on Instagram? Teenagers. Federer's appeal just isn't as big there. Ronaldo has a different target audience. Federer seems much more mature. You can use him for premium brands. Ronaldo wouldn't be credible there. But what he has is a mass appeal which is beyond Federer's reach." Tomczak is convinced that Ronaldo is cultivated as a much more targeted brand, almost like a pop star. "Federer, on the other hand, is just Federer. He's lucky there. He only has to play himself."

134 Federer's agent, Tony Godsick, takes the same view. In a 2013 interview with the New York Times, he says: "I can sell Roger Federer really well, but nobody sells Roger better than Roger." Godsick and Federer have been a team since 2005, when the latter returned to marketing giant IMG after two years of in-house management and was assigned the former manager of Tommy Haas, Lindsay Davenport and Anna Kournikova. At the end of 2013, they jumped ship from IMG and, together with wealthy US investors, founded their own agency, Team 8. Godsick knows the industry inside out and since 2000 has been married to former player Mary Joe Fernández, a former tennis wunderkind who reached three Grand Slam finals. As affable and eloquent as he can choose to be, Godsick is a steely businessman and his demands provoked a longer dispute with Roger Brennwald, the tournament director of the Swiss Indoors Basel. But his financial success speaks for itself: from 2005 to 2010, his client's income quadrupled from USD 11 million to USD 43 million per year. Godsick cemented Federer's place as a major player in the US market. When, in 2006, the latter won the US Open for the third time in a row,

Tiger Woods, fellow face of Nike and Gillette, was watching from his box. Afterwards they chatted in the locker rooms like old friends. Nobody blamed Woods for rooting for Federer rather than his countryman Andy Roddick. They were less forgiving of his infidelity.

Godsick's theory is that it's not a disadvantage that Federer doesn't have a large home market like Germany or the USA behind him: "Roger is a global icon, and we've developed his brand internationally. The fact that he's Swiss is actually attractive for large companies. Switzerland is a small country which people associate with loyalty, luxury, precision and perfection," he told Swiss daily Le Temps in 2010. "And it's as if his nationality made him a citizen of the world."

Marketing professor Tomczak agrees with the manager on a number of points: "I definitely think it's an advantage that Federer is Swiss. The country's neutrality works in his favour. He hardly has any barriers anywhere. If he were German, he could earn far more at home, but would struggle globally." More important than his Swiss passport, though, is his multilingualism, according to Tomczak: "His language skills are brilliant. I'm often in Australia in January, and it's amazing how the Australians have adopted him. That's because not only does he speak English completely fluently but is also just as funny as in his mother tongue. When Jim Courier interviews him, it's an Australian television highlight." Tomczak thinks Federer's marketing potential would have been even greater if he'd been born in the USA. The US market still towers over all the others.

Godsick of course also benefits from Federer's enormous advertising deals. The latest Forbes list of sports managers had him at USD 12.24 million per year – a respectable sum. As active as the savvy American is in marketing Federer, there is a clear concept behind it. Whereas Christiano Ronaldo collected ad deals like a football fan collecting Panini stickers – 22 new deals since 2013 alone – Federer's are long-term partnerships. Godsick once told the

story of a company who offered him an obscene amount of money just before Wimbledon 2009 if Federer broke Pete Sampras' record of Grand Slam titles (14). He declined so as not to anger loyal, long-term partners.

Federer's portfolio comprises Swiss companies with a global profile (Credit Suisse, Jura, Lindt, Rolex), or without (Sunrise) as well as global brands (Barilla, Mercedes-Benz, Moët & Chandon, NetJets, Uniqlo, Wilson). For a long time, his most lucrative deal was the one with Nike, which brought in an estimated USD 130 million between 2008 and 2018. A number of partnerships will extend beyond his active career, the one with Wilson is for life. In future, the Federer brand is to be less dependent on Federer the athlete. Brand Finance, a London-based firm which values brands, estimated his brand value at around USD 380 million after his eighth Wimbledon title in the summer of 2017. They thought he could still earn that much in advertising deals, provided his career continues for a few more years. Of course, this kind of estimate is partly guesswork, says marketing professor Tomczak. "But the scale seems reasonable to me, by all means. It could even be more." But he adds that the question remains how much Federer wants to continue his life as a brand after retirement.

It's possible that he'll then dedicate more time to the management agency Team 8, which he co-owns. At the moment it's ticking along quietly, and Godsick is tight-lipped about their activities. Next to Federer, they have the Argentine giant Juan Martin Del Potro, who won the US Open in 2009, and the young American, Tommy Paul, on their books. Bulgarian Grigor Dimitrov left the agency in late 2017, but they recently secured the marketing rights for promising young American Cori Gauff, who won the junior tournament at the 2018 French Open at just 14. In ice-hockey, the Swede Henrik Lundqvist, goalkeeper to the New York Rangers, is also a client. Rather fittingly, he's dubbed the king, like Federer – "King Henrik". But, next to Federer, the most interesting Team 8 project is the Laver Cup, which was kicked off in Prague in 2017. The concept is a copycat of the Ryder Cup, which pits the best American golfers against their European counterparts. In tennis, the current leaders, Europe, play the rest of the world. The first editions in Prague and Chicago were a big success, but it remains to be seen whether the Laver Cup can make it in the already busy tennis schedule and without Federer playing.

At any rate, Federer has often said that he finds business appealing. And as Godsick revealed to the New York Times: "I always joke with him, 'Look, you've been really successful on the tennis court, but I promise you, you'll be more successful when you're done playing tennis.'" The bar is high.

15. A million children reached – the foundation as his life's work

What do Donald Trump and Roger Federer have in common? They were both on Time Magazine's list of the 100 most influential people of 2018. Trump was in the category of "leaders", Federer one of the "titans" next to Amazon founder Jeff Bezos or Tesla head Elon Musk. The list is of course no more than a bit of fun. But Federer's nomination shows that he's long been considered more than just a tennis star. Because he wasn't nominated for his precise backhand volley, forceful serve or overflowing trophy cabinet, but rather for the philanthropic work he does with his foundation. And the laudation was penned by none other than Bill Gates. The Microsoft founder closes with the words: "Roger knows that effective philanthropy, like great tennis, requires discipline and time. It will be a sad day for all of us fans when he hangs up his racket – but we can take comfort in knowing that he's committed to making the world a more equitable place."

High praise, given that Gates and his wife Melinda run the world's largest private foundation with an annual budget of over USD 4 billion a year. Gates and Federer first met on the sidelines of the tournament at Indian Wells in 2017, where the US billionaire and tennis fan has a holiday home. At some point, they started talking about their foundations, and the Match for Africa 4 in Seattle (2017) emerged. And, a year later, the Match for Africa 5 in San Jose (2018). There, Federer faced US pros John Isner and Jack Sock, and his co-organiser Gates played celebrity doubles matches at his side. The two exhibition events brought in around USD 5 million for the Roger Federer Foundation.

Federer's tennis skills probably had less of a sustained effect on Gates – an average hobby player (speaking generously) – than the charismatic computer genius's vision did on Federer. Gates' approach is "think big". He wants nothing less than to change the world and has dedicated himself to global health and agricultural development in over a hundred countries through his foundation. It is perhaps only in the last few years that Federer has really grasped how much he can achieve off-court. And his exchanges with Gates have no doubt further inspired him in his philanthropy.

A lot of idealism and a dose of naivety were at play when Roger Federer started his own foundation on Christmas Eve 2003. He was just 22 and had celebrated his first great triumph at Wimbledon a few months earlier. During his breakthrough season he had already earned over USD 3.8 million and was wondering what to do with all the money: "It was time to think forward how much more I would like to achieve as a tennis player, but also as a human being. I am very fortunate, very privileged in my life. It's a good starting point to share that with the less privileged people in the world. The wish to give back comes from the values of my parents."

At that young age, you're usually primarily coming to grips with yourself. But thanks to his mother Lynette's South African background, he had been aware from an early age that people weren't as well off as in Switzerland everywhere. As a boy, he caught a first glimpse of **140** poverty on the African continent when travelling around South Africa on a caravan holiday with his family. And, as a side note, he has both a bright red Swiss passport and a dark green South African one. Before starting the foundation, he had discussed the idea with his parents extensively. The final impetus was winning the Baselbieter Sportsman of the Year award in 2003. The cheque for CHF 10,000 flowed into the foundation's starting capital of CHF 50,000.

Federer could have done what many do and done good by supporting other charities. But by setting up his own foundation, one which also carried his name, he made a long-term commitment. "I didn't want to just give money to different types of organisations. Then I would stand for a bit of everything and nothing. I said I wanted to do something very specific, very precise. Early childhood education in Southern Africa. It's something that really has been at the core for me. I wanted to be in control of what I do. And have a very clear message for donors and sponsors and all the people that believe in my foundation. That if they give money, which I appreciate very much, they know exactly what it is for."

The first project which his foundation supported was a school in the township of Port Elizabeth, a large South African city. There, the course was set: education as the key to an independent life. The current strategic aim is to improve the quality of education for children between 3 and 12. As of 2018, the foundation is active in six Southern African countries – Botswana, Malawi, Namibia, Zambia, South Africa and Zimbabwe – as well as in Switzerland (with charities working on poverty, supporting athletes and early education). Today, around 300,000 children benefit from the programes his foundation funds.

The Roger Federer Foundation today is a reflection of Federer himself, says Janine Händel, who has been its CEO since 2010: "When he gets to work, he really goes for it. There are no compromises. His values and convictions are followed in the foundation and he's involved in all the important decisions. There are no board meetings without him. The exchange and cooperation is intense."

Consistency and control are two key terms in Federer's tennis career, too: he doesn't shy away from decisions and has a strong handle on his team. But it took him a while to find his role as a philanthropist, as he wrote self-critically in an entry on Bill Gates' blog (gatesnotes.com) in March 2018: "I quickly realised that becoming a good philanthropist isn't easy. The will to give back is not enough on its own. In the foundation's early years, we were less rigorous about what we funded, and we quickly realised that we couldn't measure whether we were having an impact or not. If we really wanted to change children's lives in a tangible and sustainable way, we needed to go about it in a much more professional and strategic manner." He concludes: "Philanthropy, like tennis, demands time and discipline."

It wasn't just him, but also his parents and Mirka who have been very actively involved on the foundation board from the very beginning. But in late 2009, Federer came to the conclusion that it needed to be professionalised. He hired a CEO, Janine Händel, who had spent eight years working in the Swiss diplomatic service after her PhD in law, and began to set up an office in the Seefeld neighbourhood of Zurich. Today, the foundation has six employees, three of them in the Johannesburg office, the hub for the projects in Southern Africa. Federer's quiet hope that the professionalisation would save him some time was quickly dashed: since 2010, the foundation has grown rapidly, and with it, its president's workload. The sum of money flowing into its projects has increased more than tenfold – from CHF 0.72 million to CHF 7.5 million. Since 2010, the foundation has spent more than CHF 40 million helping others. In Southern Africa, it's become a well-known player with something to say.

During a four-day trip to Zambia in April 2018, Federer met President Edgar Lungu to get his messages across. He's grown so much in the role that he can easily present and debate his goals on Zambian radio for half an hour. He's a door opener. Most of the children he visits in African schools don't even know that he's a global celebrity. High-ranking politicians, on the other hand, are well aware of his star power. He can influence a Southern African country's early education policy. Beyond that, Federer never speaks publicly about current political topics. He'll never give a statement on Donald Trump or on a popular vote in Switzerland. But in his foundation's work he leverages his popularity to get things done.

At the heart of the foundation's work together with its 18 local partner organisations is the word "empowerment". The goal is to set processes in motion or to accelerate them, the CEO explains. The partnerships with local or- ganisations are long-term, and the impact is largest when the local population and their decision-makers take responsibility for the activities. Händel gives an example: "If we need a kindergarten, we don't drive up in a van, unload all the material and build it. We convince people to build one themselves. We show them how to build and contribute a bag of cement, or a bucket of paint. But the initiative and the responsibility lie with the village."

The goal, says Händel, is to create an environment which, in the long run, works without the foundation's support. Together, they build schools, train teachers, or show how a community can set up school meals themselves through the cultivation of gardens. Händel has, however, also learned that good intentions don't always make for good results. Projects can fail if the local conditions are misjudged, influential local actors are against them, or black magic comes into play. Their activities therefore need to be followed closely and the partner organisations chosen with care.

The foundation has found its purpose and may even narrow down its mission further in future to make for more targeted work and to help make its impact more measurable. In early 2013, Federer took on the ambitious goal of reaching a million children in Southern Africa with their education programmes by 2018. Their bold target was exceeded. "I never thought I was going to have such an impact on so many kids," he said. "I didn't know how active I was going to be [in the foundation]. I've realised I've got to learn that I love everything I do. I love field visits, I love the fundraising, I love meeting people, I love talking about the foundation." As tough as his knee injury was, costing him the second half of the 2016 season, it was a blessing for the foundation because it gave him the time to dedicate himself to it intensively. And since he's now even more careful with his body and plays less, he can be more active in it than ever.

Federer's "career progression into a professional philanthropist", as Händel puts it, has also meant personal development for him. The breadth of activities is a good learning opportunity for his future professional life. And the trips to Africa, where he's as hands-on as ever, are in themselves formative experiences – and something he'll have even more time for when he's not travelling the world, racket in hand.

But what about his fundraising abilities? Won't his star power wane after he retires? Händel isn't worried: "Roger's reputation has long gone beyond his sport. It's about the whole package of his personality. And when he's no longer playing tennis, he won't be dropping that. You can point to other examples like Andre Agassi and his foundation." The erstwhile eccentric from Las Vegas is extremely successful with work very similar to Federer's: he works on school access for underprivileged children in the USA and has raised around USD 185 million for the cause.

So when Federer is no longer collecting money on the court at a Match for Africa, then he might do so as a speaker or at other evening events. And the partnerships with big sponsors who support his foundation will continue. By now, the Roger Federer Foundation has also made such a name for itself that it has support from other foundations. **145** "The foundation has become a big part of my life," says Federer. "We also often talk about it with the kids. It'll be interesting to see if they're still actively involved in 20, 30 years." In other words: he's thinking big.

16. What we can all learn from Federer

I) Less is more

There's a tennis tournament somewhere almost every week, and the off-season is short. The temptation to play too much is huge. But Roger Federer quickly stood out as a rigorous planner. He divides his year into tournaments, training blocks and holidays – and when he takes a break, he switches off completely. He also doesn't accept any sponsoring or media invitations in that time. That dedication to his plans, taking the necessary breaks for recovery and holidays, is essential to his durability, helping him maintain both his body and his delight in playing tennis. And when in 2016, he found himself in a vicious cycle, his body rebelled and he lost his enjoyment, he pulled the emergency brakes and took a five-month break. On his return, refreshed and livelier than ever, he went straight on to win the 2017 Australian Open.

II) Never stop learning

Tennis is cyclical. Every great player dominates the sport with their style for a while, before they are supplanted by someone younger who knows how to respond to it. Borg was ousted by McEnroe, McEnroe by Lendl, and so on. By that logic, Federer would have had to be sidelined by Rafael Nadal, four years his junior. But he didn't let himself be ousted because he never stopped learning. He adjusted not only to Nadal, but also to an ever quicker and more physical game. It takes a lot to constantly question yourself and be open to new developments when you're that successful. Federer has managed, and so generation after generation arrive, whilst he stays.

III) Look forward, not back

Defeat is bothersome, but unavoidable. Even an exceptional talent like Roger Federer leaves more tournaments defeated than victorious. The key question, therefore, is how you deal with losing. There can hardly be anyone who manages to move past defeat as swiftly as Federer. He thinks about what he could learn from it, and then he quickly looks ahead. Others spend days wrangling with the question of which opportunities they missed, but Federer doesn't dwell on things he can no longer change. If there was one defeat which really pained him, then it was Wimbledon 2008 against Rafael Nadal. It preyed on him days later during his holiday on Corsica. But when Federer was interviewed on the 10-year anniversary of the legendary match, he had an astonishingly poor memory of the details. It's the victories he remembers, not the defeats.

IV) Love your job

Of course, Roger Federer is privileged to be travelling the world as a celebrated tennis star. But this job can get repetitive, too. You always return to the same places, play the same opponents and run through monotonous training drills. Over all these years, Federer has managed to maintain his enjoyment of tennis and delight in the job. After more than 1,400 professional matches. He's managed by refusing to let himself succumb to routine. He's stayed curious, often tries new things on the court and in 2015, even invented a new shot with the half-volley return named after him, SABR.

V) Don't take any shortcuts

As Thomas Edison, inventor of the light bulb, put it: "genius is 1% inspiration and 99% perspiration." In Federer's case, it might be 2% inspiration or a few percent more. But one thing is clear: he was only able to become so good by being prepared to work extremely hard. Again and again. The players who have joined him in training confirm it. Federer's excellent physical condition is the foundation of his tennis skill. Even he can't play winners if he can't reach the ball. There are no shortcuts to success.

VI) Channel your emotions

Passion is good, it's even a prerequisite for playing high-level tennis. But your emotions can also play tricks on you, as was the case for young Roger Federer, who let himself get frustrated too quickly when something didn't work. His emotional outbursts, often taken out on his racket, are well-documented. And when angry he played worse, not better. After a little time with the professionals he managed to channel his emotions. Since then, he only really lets his feelings run away with him after winning the match point or a tournament, often through tears.

VII) Believe in yourself

Few are blessed with the kind of talent that Roger Federer has. But he, too, had difficult phases to weather. When, from 2008 on, he started winning fewer and fewer Grand Slam titles and losing more and more to Rafael Nadal, the critical voices grew louder. There was hardly a tennis expert who didn't once say or write that Federer had won his last major tournament. But he himself never lost his belief in his own abilities, even though it was a long wait after Wimbledon 2012 – exactly 1'666 days – before he finally had another Grand Slam title to celebrate at the 2017 Australian Open. The moral of the story: even if everyone else doubts you, it's only over when you start to believe them.

VIII) Embrace the moment

Sports are a wonderful opportunity to live the kind of mindfulness which is all the rage today. You give yourself to the moment, there's no room to think about anything else. Federer is a master. When he's standing on the court, he can tune out everything else. And rather than worrying about what could happen if he loses a point, in the critical moments, he plays even better – because he manages to focus completely on that moment. As he once said, when he's under pressure, he sees everything clearly. That must be nice.

IX) Surround yourself with positive people

Roger Federer loves stability. But when he feels that something in his environment is off, he acts immediately. Like in May 2007, when he separated from his coach Tony Roche just before the French Open because he felt the Australian wasn't fully committed any more. Federer always surrounds himself with positive people who think in terms of solutions, rather than problems. Like him, the incorrigible optimist. And he found the ideal companions for his journey. He hired his fitness trainer Pierre Paganini as a teenager, his coach Severin Lüthi has been on board since 2007. His most important supporter, however, is his wife Mirka, without whom he would have stopped long ago. Her faith in his abilities is unshakeable.

X) Age is just a number

At his age, he couldn't really be the favourite, Federer joked before the 2018 Australian Open: then he went out on the court and won the tournament aged 36 years and 173 days – making him the oldest Grand Slam Champion since 1972. Since his 30th birthday, Federer's age has been the subject of considerable discussion. And time and time again he proves that it just doesn't matter to him. "Age isn't a problem, it's just a number," he said after his victory in Melbourne. His indestructability shows: it's not about age, it's about how you take care of yourself and how you feel. At 36, he plays better than he did at 26.

The Roger Federer timeline (as per March 2019)

8.8.1981	*Born in the Kantonsspital Basel*
5.7.1998	Junior champion at Wimbledon
7.7.1998	Professional debut in Gstaad
4.2.2001	First ATP title in Milan
2.7.2001	Victory against Pete Sampras at Wimbledon – their only encounter
1.8.2002	*His former coach Peter Carter is killed in an accident*
6.7.2003	First Grand Slam title at Wimbledon
16.11.2003	First of six titles at the ATP Finals
13.12.2003	*First of seven Swiss Sportsman of the Year awards*
24.12.2003	*Establishes the Roger Federer Foundation*
2.2.2004	Reaches number one for the first time after winning the Australian Open
12.9.2004	First of five successive US Open titles
16.5.2005	*First of five World Sportsman of the Year awards*
6.7.2008	After five successive Wimbledon titles, Rafael Nadal dethrones him
16.8.2008	Olympic gold in Beijing with Stan Wawrinka
18.8.2008	After 237 weeks at number one, Nadal overtakes him
11.4.2009	*Marries Mirka Vavrinec in Basel*
7.6.2009	Completes the "Career Grand Slam" in Paris
5.7.2009	Sixth Wimbledon title makes him the new record holder with 15 Grand Slam titles
23.7.2009	*Twin daughters Myla and Charlene are born*
31.1.2010	First Grand Slam title as a father, his sixteenth overall
6.5.2014	*Twin sons Leo and Lennart are born*
23.11.2014	Davis Cup title in Lille
29.1.2017	Eighteenth major title in Melbourne, the first in 1'666 days
16.7.2017	Eighth Wimbledon title, the all-time record holder
28.1.2018	Twentieth Grand Slam title in Melbourne
18.6.2018	At 36 years and 314 days, the oldest number one, with a total of 310 weeks
1.3.2019	One hundredth title of his pro career in Dubai

syntax
[sɪntaks]

We make
every language
your language.

Communication
Do you want a distinctive corporate language? We can
provide the decisive content services for you – from
transcreation to copy-editing to blog posts, ghost-writing
and professional story-telling.

Translation
Reading between the lines? Recognising cultural differences,
taking account of linguistic subtleties? Our translators can
help you to express yourself in every language like you can
in your own.

Interpretation
Do you want to translate what you say into other languages,
quickly and precisely? Thanks to state-of-the-art technologies
and the most up-to-date tools and apps, we can increase the
efficiency and cost-effectiveness of your communications.

Syntax Translations is an integrated language competence
centre. We can help you to attain a superior art of
communication.

www.syntax.ch

s y n t a x

Communication • Translation • Interpretation